3.96

2 KINGS
Walter Brueggemann

KNOX PREACHING GUIDES
John H. Hayes, Editor

John Knox Press
ATLANTA

Library of Congress Cataloging in Publication Data

Brueggemann, Walter.
  2 Kings.

  (Knox preaching guides)
  Bibliography: p.
  1. Bible. O.T. Kings, 2nd—Commentaries.
2. Bible. O.T. Kings, 2nd—Homiletical use.
I. Title. II. Title: Second Kings. III. Series.
BS1335.3B79 1983   222'.5407   82-48094
ISBN 0-8042-3214-8

© copyright John Knox Press 1982
10 9 8 7 6 5 4 3 2 1
Printed in the United States of America
John Knox Press
Atlanta, Georgia 30365

Contents

2 KINGS

Introduction

The division of our exposition of the books of Kings into two volumes is largely a matter of convenience, as the exposition in the two volumes needs to be seen as intentionally linked together. But in this matter of convenience, we follow the convention of the Bible itself. Our division of the expository material into two volumes, without good reason, reflects the division of the two canonical books of 1 and 2 Kings, also apparently done without good reason.

(A) Thus 2 Kings has no particular shape or intention unless it is linked closely to 1 Kings. Taken together, they narrate the history of Israel and Judah from the death of David (about 962) to the death of Jerusalem (587) with one episode beyond that death (2 Kings 25:27–30). To identify the two events (deaths of David and Jerusalem) and the two dates (962, 587) is to do more than to state chronological parameters. It is to suggest that these two events are substantively related to each other. 1 Kings 1–2 attests that the monarchy which continues to govern in Jerusalem is in fact a dynasty rooted in something of a coup. While that dynasty has an indisputable claim to "legitimacy" (from David in 2 Sam 6–7; 2 Sam 7:12–16 seems to anticipate Solomon and grant him legitimacy), that legitimacy is of a formal kind. But underneath the forms of legitimacy which the world accepts, one may well wonder. There is no doubt that the theologians of 1 and 2 Kings look back to the book of Deuteronomy for theological grounding, and in this respect they look especially to Deut 17:14–20, concerning kingship. In that distinctive teaching on kingship, it is affirmed that a king is legitimate for two reasons. First, legitimacy comes from being a "brother," i.e., related in the faith of the covenant. Second, legitimacy comes from reading and answering to the torah as the main clue to life. Now it takes no great insight to see that Solomon and the kings after him portrayed in this narrative are hardly formed according to the torah. From the perspective of Deuteronomic theology, with the exceptions of Hezekiah (2 Kings 18:5–7) and Josiah (2 Kings 22:2, 23:25), these kings are scarcely legitimate, according to the covenantal intentions of Yahweh and the understandings of the Yahwistic tradition. This then is a long history of illegitimate power.

It is that ambiguity that provides the main dynamic of this narrative. On the one hand, these kings are *formally legitimate*. On the other hand, these kings are *scandalously illegitimate*. And the movement of the narrative between *report* and *exposé* reflects that unresolved ambiguity concerning legitimacy and illegitimacy. That ambiguity rests on the dual inclination to judge the kings (a) according to the criteria of the nations (cf. 1 Sam 8:5, 20) or (b) according to the claims of Yahwistic faith.

Now that ambiguity in the narrative is not accidental. Nor is it because these theologians could not make up their minds. Rather it is because that is the nature of historical power. Political capacity is seen by these theologians (and by the biblical tradition generally) as ambiguous, as a way of implementing Yahweh's torah with a possibility of *obedience*, and as a sure way of compromise and accommodation which in the end is *idolatry*. None has seen this so well as Reinhold Niebuhr, first in his magisterial, *The Nature and Destiny of Man*, and then in his derivative studies on *Irony in American History*. Niebuhr is faithful to and informed by the discernment of these theologians in Kings who see that to partake of public power is to participate in this inevitable ambiguity. This literature might be usefully interpreted as a study in this very ambiguity.

Because our exposition is theological, we suggest that

this ambivalence about formal legitimacy and scandalous illegitimacy may be a focus for interpretation and preaching. The literature invites us to reflect on the ways in which this same difficult reality is operative among us, both on a large public scale, and also more personally in our accesses to social power and social influence.

2 Kings picks up the story mid-way between the death of David and the death of Jerusalem. Its beginning is more than spatially mid-way. It is mid-way in that the die has been cast. And the history of Israel–Judah is on its way toward death. Though the division of the two books may be only a convention, it is important to note that 2 Kings 1:1 begins with the death theme, "After the death of Ahab...." The whole literature is in the midst of death—David ... Ahab ... Jerusalem. This does not mean things are inevitable and irreversible. These theologians believe that until very late, until Manasseh (2 Kings 23:26 –27), there is still a chance. But the slide has begun, a slide toward death and the end. It is the slide of disobedience and illegitimacy. And we stand with the theologians watching to see if the slide can be halted and the end averted. The labored telling of the whole tale leaves the question open until the last possible moment. The theologians do not argue that it must necessarily have ended this way, nor that given another history, it always must end this way. They only tell what they see and how it was in this instant. It is a tale to the bitter end. And we cannot discern that ending in 2 Kings unless we see that the deathly inclination is fully operative already in 1 Kings (see the warning in 1 Kings 9:6–9). (It can also be argued that, taken in larger scope, the memory of Israel means to say that the movement toward death begins much earlier, already as soon as they enter the land, in the book of Joshua.)

(B) The literary and historical questions here do not need great attention, for the texts can have their own say without a great deal of critical burden.

(1) The literature, as in 1 Kings, is a shrewd and knowing juxtaposition of concrete, detailed narrative taken from many sources, now lodged in the midst of a standard, stylized, formulaic historiography. And part of our study is to observe the ways in which this juxtaposition is shaped at various points.

(2) The historical data concerns the ways in which these legitimate/illegitimate kings cope with realities that run beyond their capacity to control or even their ability to understand what is happening. While there are some debated questions about chronology (on which see B. Childs, *Introduction to the Old Testament as Scripture*, 294–300), these cannot be resolved here and do not warrant our attention, given our purposes.

These theologians have something different in mind. While we take it for granted, we should not miss that they have wrought a rather remarkable intellectual achievement. They have dared to assert that while Assyrian (and at the end Babylonian) imperial expansion appears to be the main crisis for these kings, the crisis is in fact more than that. That very *imperial expansionism* is at the same time a mode of *Yahweh's sovereign rule*. The issue is not that Assyrian power may or may not be resisted. That is what kings always think the issue is, as they ponder matters of arms and security. But the real issue is that *God is not mocked* (2 Kings 19:16). And God's torah is not voided (see Mark 7:8–9). That is the main claim of these narratives. As a king, one must not be naive about Assyria. But one must also not be preoccupied with Assyria either, because the real issue has to do with the liveliness of God, the authority of God's torah, and his insistence on God's torah, even at the risk of the dynasty, the city and ultimately even the temple. Thus the process of public history is presented as the arena in which God is mocked or not mocked. And the uncertainty which these theologians lay out so carefully and teasingly is what the public mocking of God (even by those who do not know they are mocking) does to the rule and the promises of God.

(3) These two issues go together. In terms of human history, it is the tale of *formal legitimacy and scandalous illegitimacy*. In terms of theological affirmation it is the *mocking or the not mocking of God*. And we have proceeded here making those issues the focus around which our exposition is organized. It is a peculiarly pertinent point of contact for our time. For now the issues of mocking God override all the other issues in our society. The old tired quarrels about capitalism and socialism, about liberals and conservatives, about labor and capital—all of that pales before the sense that our socie-

ty totters at the edge of collapse. We do know about living in the midst of death, even while we ourselves are enmeshed in the mocking. These texts can function as ways in which we see more clearly how the resilient rule of God has its way, now even as then. But the rule of God is always partly hidden and partly inscrutable midst the posturing of nations and the cherishing of our vested interests.

(C) We have structured this exposition around the conventional divisions of the book. The first section (1:1—11:20) continues the sorry account of the Omri dynasty and its Judaic counterpart, until the drastic turn of 842. This first section culminates in covenant making, an attempt to reassert Yahwistic legitimacy for the regime. The second unit of our exposition (11:21—17:6) is something of an interim. It seems almost like an exercise in completeness, so that there should be no gaps in the chronology. But we must see this account for what it is, or we will be tempted to imagine that this sordid recital is overly important. The practical effect of a chronological approach is that it levels everything to make it all seem of equal importance. And that is not the case, because this material is not especially important for the total movement of the literature. And then in 17:7–41, the theologians seal this part of the narrative with an unambiguous verdict. The fourth element (18:1—25:30) is a quite distinct unit. It is less complex, because now the narrative can tell an uninterrupted southern story, without needing to double back on the northern counterpart. And it also appears to be theologically the most intentional, as though now the theologians either see clearly where it will end, or at least they are prepared to share with us their discernment more candidly. This section is filled with hints that are dropped concerning the outcome.

The kings of Israel and Judah are sore tempted to autonomy, to imagining that they are free to do what they will with their power. Such a notion of course flies in the face of Yahweh's commitment to covenant. Covenant is the antithesis of autonomy. The playing out of the narrative is anticipated in Deuteronomy 8:

> Beware lest you say in your heart, "My power and the might of my hand have gotten me this wealth" (v. 17).

That is the quintessence of autonomy, and is of course the mode of most of these kings. And in the same chapter of Deuteronomy, the pay-off for such a way is clear:

> I solemnly warn you this day that you shall surely perish. Like the nations that the Lord makes to perish before you, so shall you perish, because he would not obey the voice of the Lord your God (vv. 19–20).

As these theologians present it, finally the insistence upon covenant obedience crushes those who engage in autonomy.

That issue is not one that is remote for us. And, therefore, while preaching from these texts will not be easy and will readily become abrasive, the issues of these texts are very much our issues. It will be most obvious that the texts provide important analogues to the "Arrogance of Power" present in our national life. But the issues of autonomy and self-interest in the use of power are not confined to national issues. They are present in every aspect of modern life. They have as much bearing on our personal self-understanding as they do on public policy. In every dimension of life, the odd overlay of expansionism and covenantal resilience is at work. These texts may help us discern that overlay and permit reorientation (repentance).

More Trouble
from the Same Source
(2 Kings 1:1—11:20)

This grouping of texts is a continuation of 1 Kings 17:1–22:53. It continues the collection of stories about the irresistible prophets, only now Elisha has for the most part succeeded Elijah. But the issue is still essentially the same. The *power to transform human situations* and human events is vested in these prophets who stand outside all *formal structures of power* and impinge upon those structures in free and unpredictable ways.

There is no very good reason to divide 2 Kings from 1 Kings as it is now divided. There is no natural break either in terms of history or literature. The division would seem to be at the most an accident of the transmission process. Thus 2 Kings 1:1—11:20 is in fact a continuation of 1 Kings 17:1—22:53. We make a distinction at this point in our discussion only to reflect the canonical division which has been transmitted to us.

The narrative is a celebrative reflection on the strange, inscrutable, irresistible power of the prophets. And this power is shown to impinge upon public life in Israel against conventional royal stability. The upshot of this prophetic activity is the generation of revolution against royal order (see 2 Kings 9:1–3) which finally makes possible a new covenant fully attuned to the torah and opposed to the compromising royal order (11:17).

Thus taken in long sweep, these prophetic narratives serve to advance *torah faith* at the expense of *royal order*. These narratives concerning the prophets, to be sure, are not easy to preach from, because they testify to a rationality very alien to us. But if the preacher does not become trapped in procedural and epistemological issues, it will be clear that this is richly preachable material. *The "troublers"* in Israel are the real life-givers. *The ostensible rulers* traffic mainly in hopelessness. The issue is joined between them in this narrative.

A Word Untamed, a Death Unsought (1:1–18)

Ahaziah is a nobody of a king in Israel. We were put on notice about him at the end of 1 Kings (22:51–53). Our present narrative gives one other piece of news about him. Except it is clear that Ahaziah is not really the subject of this narrative. The real news here is about the prophet Elijah. The real issue is how the king shall relate to the prophet. How shall our ability to *manage* deal with the surging lifegiving *freedom* of God's word, for the world in its freedom will not be managed for very long.

(a) The narrative is nicely framed. It begins with a sick king (v. 2). It ends with a dead king (vv. 17-18). Between the sickness and death of the king, there is a not very satisfactory interplay with the prophet. But what is clear is that kings come and go *according to prophetic authority* (v. 17). That is the function and point of this narrative. Kings are not autonomous. They cannot do what they please. They may try, but finally the prophetic word will have its say. Even if they do not know it, the kings of this earth are under another authority. The poor people of God know more and have more authority than the rulers of this age (see Luke 10:23-24)!

(b) The text is shaped with artistic wholeness. There are two rhetorical patterns which recur. The first of these is the prophetic statement which *rebukes* the king and pronounces a death sentence on the king. The rebuke is given three times (vv. 3, 6, 16). It is in fact an assertion that Yahweh alone is God. Yahweh is the only one who can give life. (Note the echoes of the contest of Yahweh with Baal in 1 Kings 18.) So the prophet raises with the king this devastating question: "What is the source of life?" The question has been echoed in the *Heidelberg Catechism:* "What is your only source of comfort and strength?" That is a preachable and urgent point. What do we look to, rely upon, wait for?

And three times there is a death sentence (vv. 4, 6, 16). The perspective is radical and ominous. Death comes to those who do not turn to the single source of life.

(c) The other rhetorical pattern is one of *royal summons* and *prophetic obstinacy.* In v. 9 the king summons the prophet in rather *complacent* fashion. He just assumes he can summons, and that the prophet will answer. But the prophet is

not one of "the king's men." Elijah's answer is a terrible
demonstration of his independent authority (v. 10). The second summons by the king (v. 11) is more *coercive*. How dare
one not answer the king! Perhaps the prophet does not understand who calls. But the response is the same (v. 12). Elijah
knows very well who is calling. In the third summons the
tone is changed. Now it is not command but *plea* (vv. 13–14).
The response is positive but concedes nothing. The prophet is
clear that his response is to God, not to the king (v. 15; see
Acts 5:29). That he has his priorities clear is evident in v. 16.
The death sentence is the same, unchanged, unretracted.

Now all of that may seem harsh. A king in need—a
prophet capable of healing, for that is not doubted by anyone
in the story. But the death sentence works its way. Nothing
of compassion here.

But this is not in fact a healing narrative. It is a political
discourse on power realities. In the beginning the sick king
imagined (as do all we "heavies") that as king he could have
his way. The point of the story (even in the book of Kings!) is
to assert not only that the king cannot command the prophet
and that the prophet "marches to a different drummer." It
asserts more, that this one who answers to another Lord is
the only one with power to announce or to avert a death sentence. That is, the power for life and death is not entrusted to
the administrators of this age, but is retained in inscrutable
ways for surprisingly unadministered agents.

The text permits the preacher to raise the issue of the
real source of life and death, indeed of the definitions of life
and death. Culture tends to confuse life and food (see Matt
6:25). The Bible surely does not acknowledge worldly authority as having legitimacy in offering definitions of life. The
Bible persistently bears witness to the ineffectiveness and ir-
relevance of those "authorities" who claim to administer life
(see Gen 41:8; Exod 18:8; Dan 2:11).

So the story warns against excessive rationality in life,
our capacity to reduce everything to manageable, predictable, controllable forms. Life is not like that. The wind blows
where it will (John 3:8). And neither law nor arms, doctrine
nor propriety, science nor technology can tame it. So the text
speaks to warn all those who have their lives planned with a
"no-surprise" future. We finally cannot have life on our own

terms. We cannot, any more than Ahaziah, summon the prophet. We cannot avert his heavy sentence. In the end, the king dies, without a single bargaining chip. And the prophet moves ahead, untamed, unsummoned, unadministered, attentive to God's free, unabashed word. Neither Ahaziah nor Nicodemus could understand. But neither could resist either.

A Man to Heaven/A Word on Earth, Dangerous as a She-Bear (2:1-25)

This narrative concerns the authorization of Elisha to be prophet. He was a disciple of the great man, Elijah, whose power and authority have not been in doubt. But how to transmit that same authority to a disciple? Conventionally this text is handled by focus on v. 11, with Elijah being taken up into heaven. And no doubt that is a crucial, irresistible event, comparable only to the seizure of Enoch (Gen 5:24), or to the ascension of Jesus. But the narrative is not much interested in Elijah and his ascent. The focus is on Elisha. And indeed the following episodes of 2 Kings depend upon the full authorization of Elisha, a man fully empowered by God, capable of unexpected well-being for the helpless and beholden to no earthly authority.

(1) Elisha is a faithful disciple of Elijah (vv. 1-7). That is a primary source of his power. The narrative attests to their closeness and Elisha's unqualified loyalty to his teacher and father (see v. 12). The testing is threefold and three times Elisha vows his utter commitment (vv. 2, 4, 6). The vow of solidarity is reminiscent of Ruth's vow to Naomi (Ruth 1:16-17) and seems to anticipate the testing of Peter's loyalty (John 21:15-17), also in a three-fold pattern.

Such prophetic figures, perhaps, do not appear *de novo*. They are taught. And they belong to a tradition. Elisha is not a new gift to Israel, but stands in and is tested by the lineage of Elijah.

(2) The center of the text concerns the transfer of power (vv. 8-14).

(a) The story is bounded at beginning and end by *the mantle* which works a miracle in the water. In v. 8, it is Elijah who does the surprise, a surprise which reminds one of Moses. Elijah works an Exodus as did his forebear. In vv. 13-14 it is Elisha who, with the mantle of his teacher, replicates the surprise, also causing another Exodus. The perfect match of the two actions testifies that the power has been fully transferred. The disciple can do what the master did. Two points should be made about this. First, it is not accidental or unimportant that the surprise is an Exodus. These are the *liberators* of Israel. And they continue to do what Moses had done, both to defy oppressive rulers and to empower helpless people. If we are to speak of "miracles," then the definitional factor of miracle is that it *liberates*. Second, it would be possible to see the "surprises" as magic. But the theological question of v. 14 precludes such an interpretation. This is not "a religious phenomenon," but *a theological assertion*. It is the power of Yahweh which comes to liberate. And these narratives assert that there is no other power which can liberate except that of Yahweh.

(b) At the core of the narrative of transition is the phrase, "double portion of your spirit." The prophet invites his postulant to ask a gift. Like young Solomon (1 Kings 3:3–14), he might have asked many other gifts. But he asks for "wind" *(spirit)*. He asks for power which blows free and unadministered (see John 3:8). He asks for the authority, even audacity to withstand the rationality and bureaucracy of the king. He asks for the capacity to work newness in a world which appears closed and fixed and settled.

The narrator has difficulty speaking about this event which defies reasonable articulation. He does not want to engage in fantasy. He also does not want to reduce this awesome event to explanations. So he uses elusive language. The important thing is not religious phenomenology, and the preacher must not linger there. It is like the New Testament reticence about the resurrection of Jesus. There is no speculation. Only a witness to the new vitality which is given and discerned.

(3) The remainder of this narrative attests to the new authority of Elisha. Three episodes speak of his new legitimation and his power to do ministry.

(a) In vv. 15–18 there is a yearning of some to check out Elijah. It is like church people lingering over the former pastor, for they have not yet let her go. They use the lame excuse that maybe God didn't get him fully away. Perhaps he is still available. Elisha in response is firm but not brusque. Finally, he lets them look, to satisfy themselves in terms of what he already knew. Of course they did not find him. "I told you so" (v. 18). There is no more Elijah. The people of God will need to move on. They will have to deal with Elisha, for he is the only one there is.

(b) The second attestation to Elisha is the cleansing of the water (vv. 19–23). The form of the story is a standard miracle pattern of trouble/intervention/restoration. The specific situation recalls Moses at Marah (Exod 15:23–25). But again there must be no speculation on the mechanics of restoration. The point is to attest Elisha. It is like the miracles of Jesus. The point is not the miracles, but only to give testimony to the person of Jesus. Elisha has the capacity to work surprises that lie beyond conventional expectations.

(c) The third attestation is an odd one (vv. 23–25). Taken by itself, it seems inhumane or silly, depending on how seriously one attends to it. But set in this chapter on authorization, with special relation to vv. 15–18 and 19–23, this incident clearly speaks about prophetic authority. There is a mockery by boys who do not know or fear his enormous authority. They are unaware that to mock God's prophet is to enter a danger zone. The word of the prophet can bring blessing, as in v. 22. But it is a dangerous word as well. The prophet is not just a friendly guy, but one taken with profound seriousness. The devouring she-bears are clearly not just an accident of the wilderness. They are agents, inscrutably summoned, to implement the prophetic word of curse. The narrators themselves do not understand prophetic authority. But they know it is awesome and one must keep one's distance. And now some others know it too, having learned the hard way. Prophetic authority in Elisha is ominous and inscrutable, and not to be treated lightly.

As with all these texts, this one is not easy to preach. But it stands as a premise for what follows in 2 Kings 3–10. It is an assertion that historical institutions stand in uneasy tension with God's will. So the text may serve to raise the question of authority both our own and the respect and disregard for the authority of others. There are rational, bureaucratic kinds of authority which are of course necessary, but which must not be taken with more than provisional authority. And there are other kinds of authority, not sanctioned by culture, but which seem to be intrinsic in their authority. That also is a dangerous authority, but it is not critiqued here. It is only celebrated and enhanced. The narrative urges that such authority can be entrusted to a successor with some continuity. This chapter forms a nice counterpart to chapter 1. There, there is an *exposé of ersatz* authority in the person of the king, whom we might credit overly much. Here there is an enhancement of another kind of authority which we are wont to minimize. It is worth recalling that Jesus' main conflicts were over his strange authority that seemed beyond categorizing (Mark 1:22–27; 6:2; 11:27–33). The crisis of authority in our culture works both ways, on the one hand, being too impressed with rationalized authority, e.g., scientists, doctors, military "experts"; on the other hand, not knowing how to assess charismatic authority which makes other, equally dangerous claims. The failure of Ahaziah in chapter 1 who has no authority and the power of Elisha in chapter 2 who has all this wild authority, is an invitation to assess how in fact life is ordered. I would not push it very far, but one can ponder the juxtaposition of the dismal, oppressive failure of the Shah of Iran and the wild authority of the Ayatollah. It is staggering to find that at least in this part of the Bible, there is one so strange and dangerous. It gives one pause.

The Water of Life, Given Beyond the Royal Water Works (3:1–27)

Again the main issue concerns the relation of king and prophet, of legitimate political authority and the unshackled vitality of the prophet. The narrative falls nicely into a central confrontation of prophet and king (vv. 9–20), bounded by a preliminary scene (vv. 1–8) and a concluding battle report (vv. 21–27).

(1) A new king means a time of uncertainty, a time in which subjugated territories can rebel (see Isa 6:1). Jehoram is a new king, grudgingly commended by the historian for some few gestures of faithfulness (vv. 1–3). And so there is a rebellion by Mesha, his political dependent. The rebellion is a serious one for Israel, for it implies economic loss (vv. 4–5). Thus the setting of the story is a military move to squelch the rebellion. The king of Israel forces his counterpart of Judah, Jehoshaphat, to go with him as ally (vv. 6–8). The willingness

of the latter so nobly expressed sounds like true friendship. Indeed, Jehoshaphat seems to have made a career of such cooperation in fighting other people's wars (see 1 Kings 22:4). Most likely Jehoshaphat's willingness reflects his subservience to the north, so that his noble response is a "command performance."

(2) But the meat of the narrative is in the middle section of vv. 9–20. The structure of this unit moves from "no water" in v. 9 to "water" in v. 20, i.e., from problem to resolution. The narrative portrays the way from "no water" to "water."

(a) The self-sufficient northern king is undone (and resourceless; v. 10). But Jehoshaphat is more resourceful. He understands that there is a "surplus dimension" to historical reality. And that surplus which goes beyond royal strategies concerns the will of the Lord, which cannot be ignored. As in 1 Kings 22:5–7, Jehoshaphat is presented as peculiarly responsive to this unadministered resource. Specifically Jehoshaphat has special confidence in Elisha (v. 12). So only now does the narrative come to its main point. But the turn is in the affirmation of Jehoshaphat. This is not wordless history. This is not history as a closed human enterprise, the shape of which is visible in newspaper reports. It does not take long for history to press the human managers beyond their resources. Life has a terror and an inscrutability that requires another word, another discernment, another act based on different resources. Clearly the narrative asserts that prophets can do for kings what kings are unable to do for themselves. Royal power is minimized here in the interest of prophetic resourcefulness.

(b) So the prophet comes with biting haughtiness (v. 13). He has no craving to be "used" for royal adventures. He resists their engagement. And finally it is out of respect for Jehoshaphat (which overcomes his contempt for Jehoram) that he agrees to involvement. The word of God does not easily enter the lists on behalf of "national purposes." The word of the prophets has other sources and serves other ends.

(c) The means of disclosure claims our attention (v. 15). The "revelation" to be given comes from "the other side." It is not common sense. It is not shrewd judgment. It is indeed a gift that lies beyond the giving of the king. It is not hard to recall in the Vietnam fiasco, protesters were silenced with the putdown, "You must respect the government, for it has more information." As it turned out, *The Best and the Brightest* did not have more information, but only a carefully constructed network of self-deceiving lies. The narrative knows better. It concedes nothing to the kings. Indeed, it assumes kings are the very ones who do *not* know. Both the *source* and the *means* of knowledge lie beyond the king. To secure state counsel by way of a "minstrel" seems odd (see 1 Sam 10:10–13; 19:20–24). But the narrative regards that as routine and is not at all interested in the process. It is mentioned only casually in passing. And as the narrative itself is not interested, the preacher must not linger here. It is enough that the disclosure comes outside "administrative" channels.

(d) What matters is the intrusive prophetic word (vv. 16–19) and its decisive result (v. 20). Though given by the prophet, it is not his word. It is God's word which intrudes and decisively alters things. It is a promise of water not given by rain, but as a surprise. And it is a promise of victory. And the conclusion affirms that the word is fulfilled.

It is this word which is the evangelical point in the text. The miracle of turning dry land to water (Isa 41:17–20) is not argued or explained. It is only asserted, for what else can one do? No means are stated, only that it is a sure resolve of God. While this is the crucial point, it is also the most difficult. How can this be talked about in a scientific context, in the reasonableness of the congregation? I do not know, except to observe that this is no new or modern problem. It must have been as ludicrous at its first presentation. It constitutes an assault on the reason and epistemology of the king. It asserts that the power of God is not confined to or defined by the reason of the king or of the culture. It asserts the freedom of God to transform situations beyond both the competence and the imagination of the king. And in fact that is all we really have to talk about. Everything short of this settles for the hopeless possibilities of the king; and we have already seen that that won't work. To rely on the king means no water. And then we are lost!

Thus there is a strange congruity between the *mode of speech* (by minstrel) and the *substance of speech* (surprising water). For both mode and substance violate the possibilities entertained by the king. Again the narrative dares to assert that the transcendent power of God is at work in the specific cases of history. And sure enough. The word is kept. Water is given. New life and victory are abruptly possible. There are two dangers in handling such a text. On the one hand, it is too much of an embarrassment and so we tend to explain and *rationalize* and make it believable. On the other hand, it is to *spiritualize* and make the agenda of "miracle" into a religious issue. But both temptations must be shunned, one as much as the other. The news here is *newness in public history.* That is a fundamental claim of the Bible, rooted as deep as the Exodus. And that claim is crucial, finally, for asserting the Easter newness which belongs in the same public world.

(3) The final episode is "mop up" action after the new gift of water (vv. 21–27). The very water given through the prophetic word is now a part of the strategy (v. 22). As a result, the victory anticipated in v. 18 is now given. The allies massacred Moab, devastated their land, ignoring ecology and even the torah (cf. Deut. 20:19–20). Moab "could not" (v. 26—see Exod 8:18). Moab is helpless in the face of God's promise.

I am at a loss to understand v. 27. It makes an important concession to Moabite religion. Perhaps it illuminates the desperate act of Ahaz (2 Kings 16:3; see Deut 18:10). Perhaps it simply recognizes historical reality. That is, perhaps in the end, the allies were beaten back and the whole episode was a failure. We are not told. The tale has a most enigmatic ending.

This text will surely be objectionable in its sanction of war by God. But that is to raise a question beyond the text itself. In the text itself, the agenda is the power of the prophetic word, the ability to break the hopeless, closed perception of the king. And that is a word much needed in our society and in the church. The more prosperous and fearful our society becomes, the more all new possibilities are measured by the computer. And the more marginal the church becomes, the more it is tempted to close itself off and rely on its habitual judgments. Against this, the text says there are "other voices," prophetic voices which must be heard because they bring news. The voices lie outside the system and come in odd, awkward and nondescript ways. And those voices which may be from God may shatter our perceptual field and transform our manifold deserts.

It remains to seek out those voices who refuse to accommodate. And this is not easy. Perchance they are the voices of the poor, of the third world, of all the "discounted lepers of illegitimacy," in our society. Perhaps it is Ertha Kitt at the White House telling Lyndon Johnson to get out of Vietnam. Perhaps it is Ramsey Clark going illegally to Tehran. Perhaps it is the caucus of the handicapped—or any of the voices we have delegitimated, now given a hearing because the royal conversation has grown boring and ineffectual. A new voice might be risked, for it is increasingly clear that, like Jehoram and Jehoshaphat, the rulers of this age do not know what to do about the energy failure.

A World Kept Abrasively Open (4:1–44)

This chapter is a collection of four miracle stories, surprises wrought by Elisha. In their original telling, they served primarily to enhance the reputation, power and authority of the prophet. That in itself does not make very good preaching, for the celebration of Elisha is not a pertinent agenda. But moving through these stories is the conviction that newness can be wrought in the midst of life which seems closed and hopeless. Newness is still at work, even though it lies beyond our expectations. Thus the text may address the deep hopelessness that moves among us when the "old truths" have failed.

(1) The four narratives have a fairly standard structure, one common to "wonder tales." It is a movement from *trouble to well-being*. And the movement from trouble to well-being is by way of *prophetic intervention*. Thus:

Trouble	Intervention	Well-being
a) vv. 1–7 poverty	intervening word	payment of debts
b) vv. 8–37 no son	promise/healing v. 16, vv. 33–35	the son lives
c) vv. 38–41 famine/poison	purification by meal	food and no harm
d) vv. 42–44 hunger	command	eating and leftovers

The form, though stated in a variety of ways, stays with this movement. And it is the dominant structure of the healing stories of Jesus, as well. He comes into a troubled situation. Jesus either speaks or acts. And things are made new. In this structuring, the point of interest is of course the mid-point of intervention. Everything hinges on that. But persistently, this is the point at which the biblical narrative is most reticent. It will not tell us how it happened. Miracles will not be "explained." And that is why we are left with no explanations, but only with stories. All that can be done is to narrate the happening, to penetrate people's imagination and leave them in amazement.

(2) The most interesting and complex of these stories is the second one (vv. 8–37). It is complex because it encompasses several crises and their resolutions. It is a much fuller, better framed story than are the other episodes.

(a) Unlike the other three episodes in this chapter, this one does not begin in petition, crisis or a cry of distress. Rather the prophet in his gratitude seeks a way to thank the woman for her kindness (vv. 11–13). And she resists. So it is the prophet's initiative to give a son, even though the woman resists a second time (v. 16). Like mother Sarah, she does not believe it is possible. That is the first intervention. Taken by itself, if the story stopped there, it could be a birth narrative.

(b) Vv. 18–31 form a plot within a plot. The child dies of a head injury (vv. 19–20). In vv. 27–28, the woman's ambivalent attitude to the prophet is evident. She turns to him only in desperation. But she is also angry that he has created this situation by giving a son for which she did not ask. The suspense is heightened by the fact that the power-laden staff of the prophet can do no good (vv. 29–31).

(c) The narrative ends, consistent with the pattern (vv. 32–37), with a resurrection, wrought by prayer and by what seems to be artificial respiration. In the end, the main plot of a son and the sub-plot concerning a dead son are both resolved.

(d) Structurally, the decisive element in each case is prophetic intervention. It is the word or act or person of the prophet which drastically changes situations which seem hopelessly closed. The church now has no more important preaching to do than to articulate that openness because the freedom of God comes embodied in such unacceptable ways.

(3) The Christian preacher will be attentive to links to the New Testament:

(a) The first episode concerns attentiveness to the *poor*. It is important that these "prophetic miracles" are not confined to physical or spiritual healing, but concern *economic* resources as well. In a recital of Jesus' wonders (Luke 7:22), the ultimate transformation, even after the wonder of resurrection, is good news for the poor (ie., debts cancelled, see Luke 4:18–19). Economic forgiveness is a crucial New Testament theme. In the listing of Luke, debt cancellation for the poor is even more "marvelous" than the resurrection.

The second episode of birth narrative and resurrection narrative is closely paralleled in Mark 5:21–24, 35–43. Along with debt cancellation, resurrection is a decisive gift, the authority to bring life where death reigns. The third and fourth episodes concern famine and food and link closely to Jesus' feeding miracles (see Mark 6:30–44; 8:1–10).

(b) It is by no means clear how we may best speak about the parallels of Old Testament and New Testament narratives. The Old Testament narratives perhaps function as *anticipations* of the Messianic ministry of Jesus. Or conversely, Jesus' acts are replications and *fulfillments* of these old memories. Either way, in both cases, what is clear is that where these events happen, the kingdom of God has drawn near. It is a kingdom which shatters the old order of misery and hopelessness.

(4) It will not be easy to preach these texts without being misunderstood. The twin dangers must be avoided, either of *explaining the stories* which cannot be explained, or of *turning the Bible into a fairy tale of archaic miracles* which used to happen, but do not any more. It will be best to tell and tell the stories as a disclosure of a new world we thought was not possible. Indeed, we have always thought such a messianic world is not possible.

It is not important to convince a congregation about miracles. But it is important to help people understand that the miracle of God's intrusive power is not just a "violation of natural order," but is a shattering of hopelessness as God's rule is asserted. The key danger for the church is to settle for a closed, hopeless world. And that will rob the church of its

power for mission, and then of its faith as well. These narratives are a mighty protest against the fixity of the world, cer-
tifying that new gifts are given. And they are given in
specific, concrete ways through identifiable historical agents.
As the church embraces such a "messianic" view of reality, it may then also look to a messianic mission and ministry.
It is the calling of the church to continue the interventions of
Elisha which bring life into a world of death.

Role Reversal: Strangers at Home, Insiders Afflicted (5:1–27)

It will be most important to take this text whole, long
and complicated though it is. To take a part of it will be to be
sidetracked, even though the healing narrative of vv. 1–14
appears to be a useful and helpful story. But taken whole, the
narrative is not about healing, but about *faith* and *the prophetic word*. It is a celebration that at the center of corporate
life stands a prophet with power to bring newness. The key
issue is to *trust the new word* (as with Naaman) or to *circum-
vent the word* (as with Gehazi). And the result: the sick man is
made well (vv. 1–14)—the well man is made sick (vv. 19–27).
Sickness and health depend on trusting God's word, and on
nothing else.

(1) *The sick man becomes well* (vv. 1–14). The first part of
the text is about a most surprising healing. It is surprising:

(a) because the story is about an outsider, not one whom
we expect to be a candidate for healing (see Luke 4:27).

(b) because the king, i.e., the normal "health care deliv-
ery system," cannot heal. Happily the king knows he cannot
do it, because *healing belongs only to God*, not to any human
agent or institution.

(c) because we are met by a *leprous stranger* and a *limited
king*. And the third surprise is that healing happens by this
uncredentialed prophet who works in such unassuming
ways. We, like Naaman, yearn to be dealt with in dramatic
and spectacular ways, but finally healing is so simple. It requires not only trust in God. It also requires trust in this one
sent from God (see Exod. 14:31).

In this exchange of the outsider and the uncredentialed
prophet, there is a delightful interaction about the "great rivers" of Syria and the puny claims of the Jordan (see Isa

8:6–8). But the Jordan, in the context of this faith, holds promise of life not held by the great rivers. Such a narrative is at the brink of magical manipulation, but it is in fact a clear and massive theological claim. No royal apparatus administers healing power, but healing power surges in surprising, uncredentialed ways.

(2) But the main interest is in vv. 15–19, an exchange which stands between the two dominant episodes. The healed man, even a military outsider, is driven to faith (see Matt 8:5–13). The main point is not healing, but *faith and its confession.*

(a) So the main issue is the marvelous affirmation of v. 15. Now the king knows. The former leper knows, deep in his body, unarguably, nonnegotiably. He knows because life has been transformed. And his knowing concerns this unique, distinctive, singular, exclusive reality of the God of Israel. Israel is acknowledged by this Syrian to bear witness to the true God. This is an affront then and now, in every time, when sophisticated people try to assert a universal God and try to banish the Jewish particularity of the biblical God. The confession of the soldier is not unlike that of the centurion (Mark 15:39).

(b) The counter theme here is that such faith is unbearable in its drastic intensity. One can come to such a deep awareness of faith. But soon it is too intense and cannot be sustained. So the military outsider promptly begins to qualify his unqualified affirmation. Those qualifications are close to our own experience. First, he has to go back home, back out of Israel where this God is not present and not confessed. So he wants a little religious assurance that tones down the danger of the confession. He still insists (v. 17) that he will serve only this God. But second, then he adds a more serious reservation in vv. 18–19. As a public man, he still must worship the national gods. He asks that he be permitted to "go through the motions," but not really mean it. That qualification is surely close to our experience, for in our public functions, all of us are called upon to make visible compromises. So there is a *noble confession,* but a *realism* about "back home." Is he ashamed of the gospel (see Mark 8:38; Rom 1:16–17)? Perhaps surprisingly the commander is permitted these reservations. It is still regarded as a valid, decisive confession. So a sermon might focus on sustaining a confession in a nonbelieving world. And we must pay attention to which compromises are permitted us.

(3) There the narrative might have ended. But it does not. In vv. 19–27 we have an added, unexpected episode. The servant of Elisha, whom we may believe is a confessor of Yahweh, seizes the opportunity. He pursues the healed man and coerces from him a "lug," ostensibly on instruction from Elisha. What he does is clearly exploitative and dishonest. And that is escalated by this further dishonesty to his master (v. 25). But Elisha, this marvelously clairvoyant man, knows better and rebukes him. It is not intended that those entrusted with healing power should exploit that power for self-gain. And thus, as a climactic statement, the dishonest servant is cursed with leprosy (27). The prophet who heals a disease can also curse with an ailment. This second half of the story is about the temptation to exploitation of special God-given healing power (see the temptations of Jesus, Matt 4:1–11, which invited Jesus to exploit his power). Such exploitation will not be tolerated.

This narrative is marvelously symmetrical. It may be preached as two tales told of every human life. One concerns *a believing outsider*, healed and sent home in realistic faith. The other is an *exploitative insider*, entrusted with faith, but who mocked the faith and brings trouble on himself. All of us know about both movements in our lives:

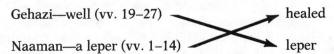

Gehazi—well (vv. 19–27)   healed

Naaman—a leper (vv. 1–14)   leper

And at the center (vv. 15–18) stands prophetic faith, a confession which the outsider accepts, which the insider betrays. The question of leprosy and healing has at its center a decision about God, God's deep demand and God's lordly gift. All parties, the foreign commander, the Israelite king, and the dubious servant all had to come to terms with the prophet whose story this is.

History Beyond All Conventions (6:1–23)

Elisha is a massive figure in the imagination of Israel, indeed larger than life. Here are three memories of the great man. The preaching possibility here is not to work with theological rationality, but to testify to this larger than life figure in the memory of the church. There is no doubt that the narrative will be misunderstood if it is taken as flat "modern" history. Then we become enmeshed in a hopeless and defensive review of "natural law" and "miracles," or we are obligated to "explain" how it really happened. The preacher will best avoid all of that and plunge the congregation into the stuff of the story. For religious energy and vitality do not come from sorting out rational categories and assessing what is "possible." Energy and vitality to be faithful are given in the bold assertion of a special memory that puts our usual categories to flight. As we give evidence of this peculiar mode of knowing, two things might happen. First it will dawn on some that we are engaged in a different rationality (not irrationality) that is not subject to the flat consensus of modernity. Second it hopefully will strike some that the stuff of Jesus in the New Testament participates in the same mode of imaginative narrative which does not argue or convince or prove or explain, but only testifies to our best memory. The clue to preaching here is to keep singularly focused on the overwhelming person of Elisha in all three episodes. And how very different everything is when this one is present.

(1) The narrative of vv. 1–7 tells a simple domestic story of Elisha's decisive presence to his band of followers. The structure of the narrative (after the setting of vv. 1–4) is simple:

(a) The *problem* of the narrative is a lost axe head, falling into the water (v. 5).

(b) At the *center* of the narrative, the great man intervenes (v. 6).

(c) The *resolution* is restoration of the lost axe head (v. 7).

That central point is expressed in a concrete, graphic, understated way: he made *iron float*. He did what could not be done. And life thus was new. "Floating iron" is an utter incongruity. Elisha deals most in such absurdities. Iron is heavy, burdensome, completely lacking in buoyancy. This man has a touch, a power that the heaviness comes alive, the dead weight soars. Life is invoked. No explanation is admitted. The reversal is like "dead/alive," "lost/found" (Luke 15:24), blind given sight (Luke 7:22). It is the breaking of a

new age in our very midst. The ultimate aim of such resurrection faith, for Elisha as for Jesus, is that the poor stand
tall. That is even more wondrous than iron that floats.

(2) In a quick narrative of vv. 8–10, Elisha is not just the
confidant to the king, but deliverer. The narrative has some
whimsey to it. It begins without precision, "The king of Syria
was warring." We are not told which king or where or why. It
ends with equal imprecision, "not once, not twice," but
countless times. It is normal and expected that this man of
God should save the king. The Israelite government is a helpless, ineffective structure, on the defensive against Damascus. But Elisha is more than an equalizer. He is the decisive
factor that tells in the battle. He is the overriding history-
maker. The Israelite king is completely dependent on him—
the Syrian king is utterly helpless before him. Political ap-
pearances do not touch the strangeness of the historical process which God keeps filled with concrete surprises.

(3) The general principle stated in vv. 8–10 is implemented in vv. 11–23. Now we have a complete narrative in which
the man of God alters the expected turn of events.

(a) The king of Syria is baffled by his inability to capture
the Israelite king. He suspects that there is a traitor or informer in his company (v. 11). He must stop the "leak" and
so he wants to tap the phones to find out. But no. The trouble
is not a traitor or an informer, but Elisha with whom the
king cannot cope. Elisha in some strange way has access to
governmental counsel. He knows what they talk about. He
prevents the war from proceeding in any normal way. So the
king sends a special regiment to apprehend the cause of trouble. The narrative makes a joke of this self-serious king,
plunging himself into such an uneven contest. He cannot win
against such a man. Every Israelite knows that, but the Syrian suspects nothing. Israel only smiles, because it knows better than the Syrians how futile is a mission against this holy
agent.

(b) Next day the Syrians have surrounded the place
where the dangerous one dwells. All are frightened except
the targeted Elisha who is a free man. His response is like
that of Jesus with his frightened disciples (Mark 4:39–40).
Elisha speaks a lordly word, redefines the situation and
shows himself the mobilizer of resources that neither Israel
nor Syria had imagined. The world of Elisha is not flat, emp-

ty or neutral. It is laden with resources given by God for
God's people. It is fear that made Israel resourceless. But
now power overcomes fear.

(c) After that decisive turn in the narrative, the conclusion of vv. 18–23 shows that Elisha, the incredible intervenor,
holds Syria helplessly in the palm of his hand. In vv.
8–18, he has saved the Israelite king. Now in his own way he
hands over the enemy into the hand of Israel. They find
themselves strangely, helplessly brought to the Israelite capi-
tol where they are in the power of Israel. The threat against
Israel has been transformed into a victory. We are not told
how. Israel need not know how. It need only marvel and give
thanks.

The resolution of the episode at the end adds a touch of
irony. The king of Israel (v. 21) clearly must obey the prophet. The prophet is magnanimous, adding a deft touch of hu-
miliation to the Syrians. Don't kill the enemy, feed them and
send them home (see Prov 25:21–22). Let them be frightened
almost to death. And then surprise them with release. Shock-
ing them is better than killing them. Now they are completely beholden to Israel for letting them live. So the raids stop.
The prophet breaks the cycle of conventional hostility by an
act of gloating generosity that disarms.

> The Syrian king has a lot to think about. The prophet
> who knows so much and seems to control is the
> one who can save.
> The Israelite king has a lot to think about. There are
> resources given to the people and prophet, beyond
> conventional politics.
> The church which bears this narrative has a lot to
> think about. Our public life cannot stay frozen in
> our little pigeon holes. Other stuff is breaking up-
> on us which leaves us amazed.

A community that knows about this inscrutable history-maker could be dangerously free of fear. The narrative keeps so
much hidden. But Israel now knows what it needs for survival, for well-being and for faith.

Outlandish Word Fulfilled by Repugnant Means
(6:24–7:20)

The ostensible problem is *the famine* (v. 25). The entire

narrative is how to cope with, survive and live through the famine. The notion of famine may or may not be easy to preach about:

(a) Some may think it remote from our well-fed cultural situation. If so the text may be too remote.

(b) But perhaps the world hunger situation has made us alive to famine. So the congregation is invited into that new awareness, which is not as far away as we prefer to think.

(c) Most of all, however, entry into this text requires touching the famine in people's lives, famine of spirit, of courage, of hope, of intimacy, of justice (see Amos 8:11–12). The crisis is the lack which presses us to diminished humanness.

(1) Entry into the story requires fully exploring the famine (6:24–32).

(a) It is deeply acute, so acute that it has led to cannibalism (vv. 28–29). That's real famine!

(b) The famine may be a theological problem, but it creates an economic crisis. It drives prices up to the terrible disadvantage of poor people (v. 25). Famine works a hardship particularly on the poor who starve first.

(c) The king is helpless to cope with the famine (vv. 26–27). The normal systems break down. And good preaching will help people see that in the deep crisis around us, conventional systems of response are defunct and cannot be relied on. The narrative presumes that the king cannot really cope!

(d) This narrative is finally not about the king, but about the prophet. The narrative places the prophet at the center. And the preaching issue is prophetic speech and prophetic discernment. The issue in famine is a prophetic sense of life. So the prophet is an enemy of the state (v. 31). And the prophet takes modest steps to protect himself (v. 32).

(2) The center of interest to be stressed in preaching is the exchange of 6:33–7:2. It consists in exchange between king and prophet.

(a) The king puts the key faith question: *"Why wait on the Lord"* (v. 33)? Why expect help from God, this one who stands outside the system and seems irrelevant? So the issue is the relevance of God to life's crises. Is God really the "help of the helpless"? It is to that issue the preacher must speak.

And the answer must not be glib. But what to do when "other helpers fail and comforts flee"?

To *Wait.* But waiting means to cease and desist, to stop our feverish ways, to break with the notion that more work on our part is the answer to human problems. The king will not wait anymore. He is prepared to act, to take matters into his own weak hands. Only, he has already conceded his helplessness (v. 27). The king defers to Yahweh. But deference to Yahweh means to let help come at its own pace and in its own way. And that is not easy for one who is prone to manage things. The preacher has a chance to bear witness to waiting on the Lord.

It means not to weary or faint,

but to run, to walk, to mount up, to have power (see Isa 40:28–31).

(b) Finally, not until now, the prophet speaks (7:1). It is a shattering, hopeful word. It breaks despair. It opens up the situation to new possibility. It addresses the economics of famine. Prices will come down drastically. Famine will end. Food will be abundant. Poor people will again have a chance. It is a word beyond the imagination of the king. It stands outside the system and assumes God will do God's own thing.

(c) In v. 2, there is a doubt. The king's captain believes completely in the standard royal solution. He dismisses the prophetic promise as nonsensical dreaming. He is exceedingly realistic. And the prophet rebukes him for his realism. Even if you do not like it, you will not keep it from happening. You simply will not share in the new gifts. So the elements of human *self-reliance, radical hope, haunting, resistant doubt* —all are present here. The king wants to be a problem solver. The prophet breaks beyond that system. The captain doubts. All these responses are a part of our ambiguous, tortured response to human crisis.

(3) Now that the issue is set, the main action of the narrative (vv. 3–15) reports the surprising way of *inversion* that the prophet anticipated, but which he had not specified. It makes one wonder how much the prophet knew—but that is futile speculation. My judgment is that the prophet did not know, had no notion of the events told in vv. 3–15. Rather he

spoke God's word of promise, trusted that word, and waited (see 6:33) for the Lord to work his word.

In vv. 3–15, we have a narrative that ought to be enjoyed as such. It ought not to be theologized, but simply told and enjoyed. It functions as a linkage of action between the *word* of vv. 1–2 and the *fulfillment* of vv. 16–20. The action is in two parts.

(a) In vv. 3–8, in a tale of lepers (of all people—utterly rejected and unqualified), we are told of the hapless, helpless plunderers entering the city and finding much food and goods from the enemy camp. It should not have happened. It was not expected. Perhaps this is an enemy ploy, a set-up. But even so, it is the secret way of the word of vv. 1–2 coming to fulfillment. The cunning tactics are a mode of God's word, even if the enemy does not know it. There is a cunning in the midst of this history over which Yahweh presides.

(b) In vv. 9–15 there is a rather odd assessment of the lepers' experience. Because of the shrewdness of the Israelite king, the Syrian ploy is exposed. What seems to be grandly fortuitous turns out to be an enemy deception. But it does not matter. What matters is that this incongruous action— enemy deception, royal shrewdness, lepers' luck—all serve God's word which will have its way.

(4) The payoff comes in vv. 17–20 which looks back directly to vv. 1–2. *The word comes to fulfillment.* The word of God overturns the famine. The will of God inverts human trouble.

(a) The primary fulfillment is stated in v. 16, according to God's promise: prices come down because of new food— poor people again have a chance. The inflationary, impoverishing cycle is broken.

(b) The secondary fulfillment in vv. 17–20 is stated negatively. The royal officer in v. 2 had doubted God's promise. The result is that he does not participate in the fullfillment. God's word will not be mocked.

The main dynamic of this text is the *question* of the king in 6:33: "Why wait for God"? The *answer* in 7:16–20 is this: wait for God because God rules and will turn situations which the king can't handle. The text invites people to reflect on the manifold famines among us. What to do? The answer given here is to wait, to listen, to believe God's promise

which may be fulfilled even by "worthless lepers." Such a text joins sharp issue with our cultural ideologies which,
- (a) deny there is a *famine*,
- (b) trust the power of the *king* to cope,
- (c) ignore the plight of the *poor*,
- (d) doubt that prophetic *word* makes a difference.

But finally the text speaks about waiting, hoping, expecting, trusting. It speaks about God's strange attentiveness to the poor, the use of the "worthless" for newness, and a future which lies beyond the competence of the pitiful king.

Four Notes on God's Troubled Way Through Israel's Darkness (8:1–29)

This chapter presents a miscellaneous collection of four individual narratives. The whole appears to function as a connection to major narratives, or as a transition to the next major episode.

(1) The brief narrative of vv. 1–6 concerns the status and welfare of a helpless, powerless woman, whom we have already encountered in chapter 4. The structure of this narrative is simple, but important:

(a) There is a *beginning* (vv. 1–3). The woman has been out of the country among the Philistines to escape the famine. Her property was confiscated by the crown. She comes back landless, bereft of standing in the community. She petitions for the crown to return her property to her. (In passing we may observe that in the narratives, often the issue is the matter of property which the citizens have lost to the crown.)

(b) In vv. 4–5 there is an *intervention*. Gehazi, aid to Elisha (see 4:19–27), petitions the king on behalf of the woman. In other narratives he is not so noble. But here he makes a risky intervention. It is especially important that in these narratives, preoccupied with royal power, the prophets persistently attend to the poor. And that concern radically changes how royal power is understood, at least in these narratives.

(c) In the *conclusion* of v. 6, the intervention is successful. The king restores to the woman her full property and rights.

The structure of *helplessness, intervention, and restoration* is a classic form of "miracle narrative," reflected as well in many of Jesus' actions. The main point is that the intervention causes a real and decisive transformation in an economic situation. And there is no hint that the king, for all his royal standing, can resist that economic intervention.

(2) In vv. 7–15, we are offered an odd encounter with a Syrian prince, son of the king. It is most important that an Israelite prophet concerns non-Israelite political power. The prophet addresses "the nations" (see Jer 1:10). Indeed in v. 9, the king is "your son" to the prophet, meaning accountable to him, derivative from him and fully deferential to him. It is an enormous concession, even if it is only courtly style. Two elements in the episode may be noted.

(a) The agenda of Benhadad is life and health. Strangely the prophet dissembles. He sends a message of health (v. 10), but he knows the outcome is death, death and not health. And, in fact, that happens. In v. 14, health is announced, in v. 15, death comes. We are not told why there is this contradiction. The most we can observe is that the prophet presides over the king, seems to hold the power of the future in his hands.

(b) Inside that exchange, the prophet addresses Hazael, the crown prince. Like Jesus weeping over Jerusalem, Elisha weeps in anticipation for the evil and inhumaneness yet to come for this cruel regime (v. 12). The prophet witnesses a striking juxtaposition of *power in the face of kings* and *pathos for victims*. This same juxtaposition is evident in Jesus who is unyielding before *authority*, but deeply moved by the plight of the *powerless*. Thus Elisha anticipates the indignation of Amos' account of Damascus (Amos 1:3–5).

(3) In vv. 16–24, there is a summary of the reign of Jehoram, king of Judah (in v. 23, called Joram). The report is stylized and unexceptional.

(a) The *historical data* concerns revolts of Edom and Libnah. Nothing is said about reasons, but one may surmise that there was oppression and exploitation. And the drive for freedom will not finally be resisted.

(b) The theological point is made in v. 18: "He did evil . . . yet! . . . " He had to pay for his evil. Yet—God protected him not for his merit, but for God's gracious promise to David (see 2 Sam 7:14–15). God's promise impacts public life. Evil makes a difference, but evil is not the last word. The last, best word is God's own word to David (see Isa 55:3). Perhaps the preachable point is that the Bible (and especially prophetic faith) lives in the real world of power, injustice and freedom. But prophetic faith does not assume that evil in history can finally preempt God's purpose. The book of Kings is realistic and must not be made religious. But it is a special kind of realism which challenges the technical reason among us that passes for realism.

(4) In vv. 25–29, we have a brief summary note on the political alliance of north and south. The note affirms the alliance, comments on the evil and speaks about the sickness and healing of Joram. We are not dealing here with stick-figures, but with kings who must live daily, personal lives. Perhaps most important here is the ominous reference to Athaliah (v. 26). She looms as an alien, threatening force in narratives to come. The historian here hints at the dark side of Israel's history and its sorry way to self-destruction. It poses in a quite understated way this question: Why must historical actors resist the gift of life God would give? That is an overriding question for this literature.

Hopeful Word/Dangerous Coup/Painful Memory (9:1–37)

This chapter is a crucial one for this version of the history of Israel. It is also decisive for articulating a philosophy of history. It is a candid political narrative which moves at the level of coup—treachery, treason, assassination, and usurpation. That is how it is in the real world. And that is how it must have happened with this people. But at the same time this is an ominous theological statement about the dark movement of God's irresistible power which both raises up and brings down (see 1 Sam 2:6–8; 2 Sam 3:1; Luke 1:52–53). The main point of preaching here is not the specifics of the narrative, but this overlay of theology and history which attests to real shifts in worldly power. One may hope that Christians in our culture might learn to read our own time with this bi-focal agenda. With African liberation, the Palestinian urge for land, the radicalness in Iran, the threat of oil, the surge in Poland, what may be happening before our eyes is a deep shift in world power. And it frightens us because it may be a shift away from us. There is no doubt that this power shift comes out of a mixture of motives—greed, yearnings, dreams, angers, etc. But this view of history argues that as surely as invisibly, God's purpose moves in the process. And that purpose moves firmly, even savagely, to right wrongs. Christians may learn from texts like this one not to dismiss upheavals in terms of *Realpolitik*, but also to attend to the dark ways of God.

(1) In vv. 1–3 the initiative comes from God to the prophet. History is made new. Old structures are shattered by prophetic presence. It is put baldly. God authorizes a coup. Neither God nor prophet assumes present forms of power and legitimacy are fixed and settled. Our most precious power arrangements are dangerously challenged by God's will for new power configurations. And this is a narrative about such challenges and new configurations wrought by God.

(2) In vv. 4–13 the prophetic instigation is given political concreteness. Dramatic protest action is taken in obedience to prophetic instruction. Notice, all without political legitimacy! Prophetic faith can impinge upon political realism. And one agenda of the church may be to foster such an awareness, that such acts which lack the *political legitimacy* of the process may have *theological credibility*. It is a frightening prospect for us. And the upshot is the mobilization of political support in the barracks (v. 13). Aside from prophetic instigation, what happens here sounds strangely and embarrassingly like an average military coup.

(3) In vv. 14–20 there is a paced telling of the details of the conspiracy. While the narrative may be most interesting and action-filled, in fact it is a pause in the intensity of the drama. Under scrutiny, nothing happens here.

(4) The pay–off of what was begun in vv. 1–3 comes to fruition in vv. 21–30. This includes the assassination of Joram, king of Israel (v. 24), Ahaziah, king of Judah (vv. 27–28), and Jezebel, queen mother (vv. 30–37). So the political conspiracy moves unflinchingly to its "success." All of that was already implicit in the initial charge of v. 3.

But we have not yet reached the deep claim of the narrative. It is signalled in v. 21, "meet at the property of Naboth." With this reference, the story teller brings all the freight of 1

Kings 21 into this story. From that story, left unresolved, comes a special passion for "little wronged people." A massive threat against the dynasty has been lingering all this time. What comes clear is that history has enduring entwinements. There are sowings and there are reapings over a long period of time. The God who governs history has a long memory. Soon or late, there is a settling of accounts. And so the promises of God (threats) made in 1 Kings 21:19–24 are now mobilized. So the preachable question may be: what are the unkept promises and unfulfilled threats now at work in our public history? Does God have that long a memory? The narrative affirms that the historical process is not a series of unrelated, discreet "time-frames" which successively become "inoperative," but the historical process is a flow of purposes and counter-purposes which transcend specific plans and individual decisions. So we may observe this *overplus of purpose* which is decisive for history:

(a) The king wishes *shalom*, disregarding the past (v. 22; see 20:19, where another king, Hezekiah, disregards the future for the sake of present *shalom*).

(b) The usurper expresses a deep indictment of the king (v. 22). The king is accused of harlotry (mixed loyalty) and sorcery (manipulation of the power of public life). The regime has not kept faith with the God of Israel.

(c) Jehu gives closure to the interview by linking the assassination to the unrequited blood of Naboth (vv. 25–26). And all according to God's word!

(d) The narrative reaches its conclusion (vv. 36–37) with a direct reference to 1 Kings 21:23. The king is helpless before the overarching rule of God.

And there it ends, with the terse formula: "This is Jezebel." The queen mother is made a public example of people with power who believe they are autonomous and not bound by the rule of God.

Out of the narrative emerges a powerful historical–geographical symbol to which Hosea returns a century later: Jezreel (Hos 1:5; 2:22).

Entry into this text might be made by noticing the power of such a *place with a memory*. Jezreel serves in the Bible to discern history as having its own enduring purpose. And those who violate or ignore that purpose will be crushed. So Jezreel plays deep in Israel. And we have counterparts: Valley Forge, Lexington-Concord, Gettysburg, Vicksburg, Dunkirk, Pearl Harbor, Hiroshima, Me Lai, Selma, Kent State. Each of these links the present to the past. Each of these bespeaks unsettled debts and unresolved promises. Each is sure that history is governed by one who will have his way and not without hurt. These places are places that wait for an answer. The anguish and the hope linger, waiting. The waiting can be for a long time, because the place does not forget. Hurt must need happen in history, because God's way finally will not be mocked, evaded or nullified.

Ruthless Loyalty but a Mixed Result (10:1-36)

This narrative is a crucial one for the book of Kings, and for the history and faith of Israel. It celebrates a decisive break in the history and religion of Israel, implemented by the usurper Jehu, but instigated by the prophet Elisha (see 7:1-3). So it warrants attention. But it is also a difficult text from which to preach, both because it is so complex that it will take great effort to get the story straight, and because its claims are so alien to our modern consciousness.

The narrative is about a coup wrought with military finesse and cunning, but with enormous theological freight assigned to it. The coup itself is the main point, in which the rulers are killed and their religion nullified. Perhaps in a stable culture such as ours, it will be important for this text to have its say: God is not simply on the side of established order. Our most precious ways of peace and prosperity are always jeopardized by the rule of God. We live a jeopardized life. And this narrative urges at least that we do not settle the jeopardy too easily or unambiguously. And even if the coup of Jehu did not fully work out as hoped, it is, according to the text, unambiguously willed by God.

In a very different mode, the same jeopardizing of our system of peace and prosperity is the central New Testament claim. That is evident in Jesus' first statement about the new kingdom which displaces the old kingdom (Mark 1:14-15). It is the unambiguous claim of radical anticipation of a displacement of kingdoms (Rev 11:15). To be sure, every historical effort at such a radical alternative is less than

anticipated. But in such upheavals which threaten, the Bible
dares to believe the public purposes of God are at work. Such
a study of public power and public hope may be important in
our time with the rise of the third world, and the enormous
fear of the first two.

(1) In vv. 1–6, Jehu advances his revolution by shrewd
intimidation. He sends an ultimatum to the aids of the king
(vv. 1–3). He has already killed the king of Samaria
(9:21–26). The intimidation works. The aids surrender (vv.
4–5). And he requires public evidence, for he is a suspicious
man (v. 6). Thus far, not any blood shed here.

(2) The public evidence of capitulation is given in vv.
7–11. The entire royal entourage has forsaken the dynasty
and come over to the usurper. After all, for such public functionaries, the main thing is to back the winner. Beyond such
survival, which king rules is a matter of indifference. It is not
a matter of principle to prefer one tyrant to another. But the
preachable point (clearly intended to be so by the narrator) is
in v. 10. There it is affirmed that Jehu's actions not only have
a divine sanction, but they are in fact simply the working out
of God's word of promise, already spoken against the dynasty
of Ahab. Thus the verdict of Elijah (1 Kings 21:21–24) is
again decisive. Indeed that one assertion is the propelling
force for all of this history. The intrigue against Naboth in
that chapter had already fixed the end of the dynasty which
Jehu now supercedes.

Now a suspicious interpreter might guess that Jehu's
speech in v. 10 is propaganda, and perhaps it is. But that is
not the claim of the text. Rather it is claimed as the truth.
And the truth is that history does not consist in the little
strategems of kings and servants. All of that is set in the
midst of God's sure intent which will not be resisted. Indeed
once such a word is given, no royal device can turn it away.
It is this inexorable power beyond bureaucratic comprehen-
sion that so bewildered Pilate in his discernment of truth
(John 18:38). And so for us in our modernity, it is the same.
We imagine we govern history. We speculate about oil and
nuclear power and cold war. We play the "China card." And
here it is claimed that God has spoken his word and watches
over his word to bring it to fulfillment. And none can turn it
back (see Isa 14:24–27)! So the text bears witness to the pur-

poses of God which move in such hidden, yet sure ways. We might wish for a match-up of that sure word with something better than Jehu. But that is how God works. There is transcendent power and there are earthen vessels. Jehu is a rather sad earthen vessel, but the transcendent power will have its way (see 2 Cor 4:7).

(3) In vv. 12–17 two quick episodes are placed together. Negatively (vv. 12–14) Jehu kills members of the southern royal family. The narrative hardly notices this bloody act. The stakes are high. Jehu ruthlessly consolidates his power. No serious revolution could bother with compassion.

Positively and in curious juxtaposition, Jehu publicly receives the support of Jehonadab the Rechabite (vv. 15–17). The Rechabites must have been a sect-like group (see Jer 35) known for its unqualified and uncompromising loyalty to Yahweh. Frank Frick has proposed that it was not a religious community but a professional guild. But even so, its religious commitment is clear. Surely its support was important to Jehu, for his bloody movement depended on such harsh, rigorous theological legitimacy. The text is not a sanction for mass killing, even in the name of religion. But it does question our bourgeois modes of toleration. Yahwism, soon and late, is an intolerant movement. So the flag word is "*zeal for Yahweh*" (v. 16; see 1 Kings 18:21; 19:10, 14). The text raises questions about indifferent toleration which is unable to distinguish Yahweh's will from civil religion. Perhaps the text hints at the hard and tempting place where true faith must always live, between a *careless toleration* which won't sort things out and a *misguided zeal* which too easily equates God's way and ours.

(4) The high drama of this narrative is in the public gathering of devotees of Ahab's Baalism (vv. 18–27). This narrative evidences that the coup finally has a theological agenda. The change of kings is nothing if there is not also a shifted loyalty.

(a) The gathering is done by subterfuge (vv. 18–24). Jehu poses as a loyal Baalist in order to get all the practitioners in one place at one time. Like a rhetorical assault, the term "*baal*" occurs here eleven times. Care is even taken to exclude any Yahwists from the meeting. The ideological purity of Jehu is undoubted. And that is a preachable point. It must be remembered that the trigger for all of this is land-seizure in 1 Kings 21. This Baalism, a fertility religion, is not concerned simply with religious rites, but it has clear, secular socio-economic implications. The decisive critique of baalism, ancient or contemporary, is its self-serving economics legitimated by uncritical religion. And when one considers the "slide of history" against American affluence now under way, one can at least ask the extent to which this is a move from on High against a self-serving economics, legitimated by uncritical fertility religion.

(b) The ploy works. The destruction is complete (vv. 24b–27). The visible symbols are destroyed (see Deut 12:2–7). The followers are eliminated. And as if a final mocking, the theme of reversal is ultimately that the *shrine* has become a *toilet*, the place of worship is used as a place of contempt (v. 27). This is an exceedingly harsh narrative. It will not play well in much of the church. But it reminds us of the kind of literature we have on our hands in the Bible. This is not pleasant, accommodating literature, but a harsh, confrontive assertion. The threat of Yahwism is always against every self-satisfied ordering which violates some for the gain of others. The function of this literature is not to mobilize folks to public revolution. But it is to invite people to alternative perceptions of reality, to look again to see the odd configurations of power, wealth and belief into which we have fallen.

(5) There the narrative ends. The coup is total. And there the old memory ends, simply and unambiguously. But the old memory is now handled by a subtle, reflective theologian (vv. 28–36). That theologian has more distance, and in perspective he sees that Jehu is not quite the way the old memory wanted him to be. So a sober response concerning this brash rebel is added.

(a) There is a double qualification on Jehu (vv. 28–31). After all this public acclaim, one can see:

> v. 29: *"But,* he did not turn aside . . ."* He did well, but he still practiced some of the same tempting self-serving of his predecessors.
> v 31: *"But,* Jehu was not careful to walk in the torah."* He found it too easy to compromise and accommodate.

(b) So there is an almost tragic closure to the narrative (vv. 32–36). Even this most zealous one did not turn the tide. So land-loss has begun: "Yahweh began to cut off parts of Israel." The erosion of well-being, the collapse of property and security, and Israel is on its way down-down-down. So there is a pause. And the preacher may invite the congregation to pause:

(i) over *accommodation* that surely will be judged;
(ii) over *zeal* which is true zeal;
(iii) over zeal which none the less *serves itself* in the end.

And through it all, the well-being of baalism, the thinness of the Yahwistic revolution, the passion of the instigators, the public cowardice of the servants, and the public support of the sects, all that may give pause—to ask how inscrutable is God's way. For all our best efforts, how far our ways fall short of God's will (Isa 55:6–9, Prov 19:21). Well-off Americans are invited to a pause, and perhaps a re-reading of our memory and our hope. Are the *accommodators* and the *purists* all together destined for land loss?

New Covenantal Beginning—Only with Hard Risk (11:1–20)

The discontinuity in public life caused by Jehu in 842 B.C. (cf. chapter 10) was deep and massive. The main action was in the north, Jehu's own sphere of influence. But along the way, he had leveled the royal family of Judah (10:12–14). The historian has a concern for continuity in the midst of such disruption. But the continuity cannot be just any old continuity. It must have legitimacy. The present chapter concerns *illegitimate continuity* (which is unacceptable in the form of Athaliah) and *a new beginning* (in the young king Joash) which had a thread of continuity.

(1) Athaliah is no real claimant to the throne (vv. 1–3). She is a queen mother whose main roots and perceptions came from the northern dynasty (8:26). Something of a southern Jezebel, she continues the very Baalism against which Jehu had mounted his purge. She is a part of that old, unacceptable order. Taking pains to consolidate her illegitimate rule at the expense of her family, she is the paradigmatic villain in the presentation of this historian.

(2) The heart of this narrative presents the conflict of legitimate and illegitimate claims to power (vv. 4–16).

(a) The dynasty of David appeared to be ended. Only Athaliah remains. And she is no member of that dynasty. So the historian poses the dramatic question: what now for the dynasty? What now for the promises of Yahweh made long ago (see 2 Sam 7:11–16)? Because of the care and insight of the faithful priest, Jehoida, there is yet an heir to the dynasty (vv. 4–12). The young boy is a surprise to those who, like Athaliah, relished the end of the dynasty. He is equally a surprise to those who grieved its ending. But there is an heir, nearly as surprising as Isaac (Gen 18:1–15; see Heb 11:12), as providential as Moses protected (Exod 2:1–10; see Heb 11:23). There is new hope for this people.

In great detail a new beginning is reported by way of coronation (v. 12). It is a maximum security operation, for it is an act defiant of Athaliah, and undoubtedly by her lights, an act of treason. An act of *fidelity* is here perceived as an act of *treason*. The boy of course is a danger, for he threatens the crown (see Matt 2:16). And the planning committee must proceed carefully, for they also are at risk of life. But the new crowning succeeds. History does begin again. New life is possible. Society cannot long or safely endure without legitimacy.

(b) But of course the new king is not only welcomed. The new king is a threat (vv. 13–16). And so Athaliah, sensing the loss of her illegitimate power, joins issue with the label "treason" (v. 14). But the revolution does not flinch. The pretender is executed on royal order as a threat to legitimate power. The last remnant of the old regime is eliminated. The Bible is exceedingly realistic. It knows that in the building of a new order, decisions must be made. Compromises are costly. The tense issue of legitimacy/illegitimacy, of luke-warmness (Rev 3:16), of "two opinions" (1 Kings 18:21) finally must be faced.

(3) But all of that—intrigue, security, execution—are all preliminary to the main act (vv. 17–20). Now it is *covenant time*. It is time for legitimation, time for public agreements and reorientation. This moment of covenant-making seeks to reconstruct the public order after a time of rebellion and ille-

gitimacy. In the sweep of Israel's faith, it is an act as decisive as the events of Moses (Exod 24:3–18), David (2 Sam 7:11–16), Josiah (2 Kings 22–23) or Ezra (Neh 8–10). It is a decision that a new beginning in fidelity can be made. It is possible to move on in history. New beginnings can move past old failures. The covenant is a rich and bold act:

(a) It is a fresh decision *to be God's people* (v. 17). It is nothing less than a recharacterization of Israel. This is a community which had taken its life in its own hands. Now it resolves again to live from the gifts God gives. This is a community which had devised its own norms. Now it resolves again to heed the torah. The preaching point is nothing less than *the church reformed by God's word*.

(b) The covenant is not only theological and ecclesiological. It is also *political*. The covenant includes "horizontal" agreements about power between king and people. Thus the alien institution of kingship is radically redefined by this most crucial Israelite practice (see Deut 17:14–20 where kingship is subordinated to torah). The *redefinition of civil order* is a bold theological act. Authority is now made legitimate but also provisional.

(c) The covenant requires *a break with non-covenantal modes of reality* (vv. 18–19).

And those non-covenantal facets of life include worship, but also economics. It is the "people of the land," the peasant folk, who celebrate the new order. So the question is put about *breaks* with non-covenantal modes of community into which there is this liberating intrusion.

(d) The end is joy (v. 20). The narrative which begins in brazen exploitation ends in faithful celebration. Evil in history is overcome, albeit in ways not romantic.

The text asserts to the church that *new beginnings* built from *old promises* are possible. And this is both an old promise (to the family of David, 2 Sam 7) and a new beginning in the person of the young king and the ceremony of covenant. But the new beginning requires and depends upon bold, risky action which *rejects* as well as *embraces*. There can be something new under the sun. But it entails not flinching from the costs of historical choice.

A Rush Toward Death—
Unwitting
(2 Kings 11:21—17:6)

These chapters are an "in-between" section for this theological historan. In the structure of the historical narrative, the account moves from *the new covenant* (11:1–20) to *the negative theological assessment* (17:7–41). The narrative between contains interesting material, some useful for preaching. But it makes no major theological advances and serves primarily to fill out the chronology of the two kingdoms. In our discussion, this material is dealt with briefly, because we do not think it especially important. It is obvious that many points merit a more extended consideration, but some choices must be made. On the whole this recital is rather like mastering the dreary season of American presidents between Andrew Jackson and Abraham Lincoln. In that history, because of Calhoun, Clay and Webster, the real history-makers are not on the presidential list. One suspects the real history-makers in Israel are not on the king list either.

(1) Jehoash reigned forty years, a long time (2 Kings 11:21–12:21). But his crucial act of new beginning has already been reported in 11:1–20. In theological summary he receives an ambiguous evaluation (12:1–3: He "did right . . . but . . ."). The theologian knows about historical ambiguity and recognizes its recurring presence. These kings are at the same time *faithful but fickle* (shades of Luther, *simul justus et peccator*).

(a) The main issue reported is repair of the temple (12:4–16), a standard royal act in the ancient world, one important to Judah (cf. Hag 1:9–15). Public faith needs gestures of public fidelity. Perhaps it is worth linking this to Jesus' radical self-understanding about himself as the new temple (John 2:13–22). Even in the narrative on temple repair, there is political realism. For clearly there is some subtle negotiation with the priests at work here.

Here and at other crucial points in the narrative, there is an acute interest in the temple. It is for sure that the narrator had such an interest. And it is likely that the "characters" in the story, i.e., the kings, did in fact care that much about the temple. Consideration of the temple is important not only because it is visible in the narrative (see Josiah's temple reform, 2 Kings 22). It is important because "temple" symbolizes our best attempts to give our faith centrality and visibility in public life.

First, one may observe some reasons why the theologians pay attention to the temple. It had been the primary occupation of kings in the ancient world for a long time. Maintenance of the temple was crucial for the maintenance of the throne. For Israel, the temple is central because of the place and role of the Jerusalem temple for the life of faith. It is the embodiment of Yahweh's commitment to the Davidic house (see 2 Sam 7, Ps 132) and it provides a guarantee of God's presence in and patronage to Israel (see 1 Kings 8:12–13). Israel's hymnody is crucially committed to the temple, not just as a cultic act, but as a profound theological conviction (Pss 84:1–4; 122:1–9). Most of all the temple is important because it gives body to Israel's hope that some day God's rule will be fully established over all of creation, for a shelter (Isa 4:1–6) and for a program of peace (Isa 2:2–4). The temple bears witness to that governance not yet established but fully promised. John Bright ("Haggai Among the Prophets," *From Faith to Faith*, ed. by D. Y. Hadidian, 228) identifies that dimension of temple faith:

> Prepare for his coming! Build his house! Act in the light of the promises! Don't worry that you are unable to build a very fine house! Build! Act! For how can you expect your God to come to you, rule over you and bless you, if you refuse to do the necessary to prepare for his coming?
> So the temple *had* to be built. But this was not that the community might have a fine church in which to worship, and of which to be proud. It was not even that it might regain a sense of its identity, or once again enjoy prosperity. It was the act of faith by which God's people prepared for his eschatological coming in glory.

In these comments Bright speaks about Haggai in the postexilic period. But these hopes are not new in the sixth century. They are held earlier, in the generation of Jehoash. The king cares for and nurtures the deepest yearning and the best hopes of Israel for a life fully reconciled with God. Public religion matters, because it shapes, appeals to and creates public imagination.

But second, we are required, as we look at this text, to look beyond it. We know where the story is leading. It leads unflinchingly *to the reform* in 621 (2 Kings 22–23) and then immediately, *to destruction* (2 Kings 24). These theologians know the temple is crucial. But they know more. They know that the temple is not the last word, but the next to last word. Josiah knows that later on. He is repairing the temple. But the finding of the torah scroll takes priority and quickly supersedes the agenda of the temples. That sense of priority dominates this whole history. King and temple are *consolidating institutions*. But torah is a *protest institution* that moves characteristically against the social establishment. Both the king and temple on the one hand and the torah on the other hand, are present in our life. Both warrant our attention. Our lives and our community need a practice of faith which both "tears down" and "builds up" (Jer 1:10). But in this literature, informed by the torah tradition of Deuteronomy, there is no doubt which is decisive.

And of course that same tension is resolved in the same way in the New Testament. There is no doubt that Jesus is the Lord of the temple. But it is equally the case that when the chips are down, on the Friday of his death, the temple is overcome and destroyed, displaced by the rule of this scandalous one. Thus the theologians share in this judgment with the New Testament. The temple is a conflicted symbol. It is both valued and judged, constructed and destroyed.

In some ways Jehoash (and all kings like him) play at best a penultimate role. He is apparently devout. What he does is not unimportant in relation to the temple. But his action does not touch the basics. And when temple reform does not touch torah obedience, there is a temptation to recast religion into a buttress and support for the present civil order. Kings are tempted to "wrap themselves" in the temple as in the flag. Jehoash surely did not discern this problem, as we often do not, but that makes it no less the case. It is evident that his temple enterprise provided no adequate ground for the political crisis which immediately followed (vv. 17–18). Political realism contributes to the dismantling of the very religious enterprise to which he was devoted. So when pressed by political necessity, he does not hesitate to "borrow" from the temple to which he was so greatly committed. Preaching on this text may explore the need both that temples be erected and that temples be destroyed. There is need to organize public life around such symbols. And there is need to criticize such symbols, which always are tinged with self-interest. The temple may be reformed. But the Lord of the temple is not much fooled or delayed by such busyness.

(b) While temple repair is of great interest, the brief note of vv. 17–18 indicates things are not well. Tribute money (protection money) sent to Syria shows Judah's weak position. And worst of all, it is *temple revenues* that are sent. Even *temple claims* addressed to the holy God are sacrificed to *political survival*. Is this a confusion of priorities?

(c) The last note of vv. 19–21 again shows realism. This initiator of the "new Israel" is rejected (see 11:17). Perhaps there is a conspiracy because of his failure to "maintain nuclear superiority over Damascus." In any case religious effectiveness is not enough to hold the throne.

(d) Worth noting, even if beyond the text, is the parallel version on Jehoash in 2 Chron 24, a very different version. Reference to this might be made as a hint of how "revisionist" is biblical narrative. That text indicates (i) it was the old priest Jehoida, who kept the king faithful (2 Chron 24:17–19). And at the death of the priest come all kinds of infidelity; (ii) that even the king helped eliminate a prophet (son of Jehoida) who insisted on radical faith (2 Chron 24:20–22); (iii) that Syria was a most dangerous threat so the king was preoccupied with survival (2 Chron 24:23–24); in vv. 25–27, the reason is given for the assassination of the king. The version of Chronicles may be more theologically intentional. Together the two versions indicate how ambiguous is this faith that tries to live openly midst the realities of political power.

(2) Chapter 13 summarizes materials on the north. This is fairly straight power politics, with an overriding awareness of the Syrian threat.

(a) Jehoahaz, son of the usurper Jehu, is in a vulnerable position (vv. 1–9). He is reduced by Syria to be a weak, dependent neighbor. The high promise of Yahwism has not worked in the political arena. There is a quality of *political unreality* about this *radical faith*. It leaves open all the issues of how to be *in* but not *of* the world. Of special note is the comment of vv. 4–5 which reflects the theology of the book of Judges: cry to Yahweh—receive a savior (Judg 3:9, 15).

In vv. 2–5 we are offered a remarkable summary of the parameters of the theology that governs this history. It is well known that this fourfold formula governs the book of Judges, cf. e.g., Jud 3:7–11. But it is remarkable that the same theology occurs not only in the book of Judges, but in the book of Kings. Apparently the institution of monarchy does not change the theological realities even a little bit. The same theology is laid out clearly:

(i) The king does evil (v. 2). The evil he does is to imitate Jeroboam who is remembered as a syncretist who does not rely on Yahweh.

(ii) The assured consequence of such mistrust of Yahweh is God's anger and then judgment (v. 3). As in the book of Judges, that anger takes the form of political and social oppression, this time at the hand of Syria.

(iii) A major turn in the narrative and in the reported posture of the king is that he turns again to Yahweh (v. 4). He seeks the favor of Yahweh, because he has at long last discerned that the favor of the other gods, and consequently of the Syrian overlord, is not much comfort. This means, for the narrator, that the king has abandoned his syncretistic practice and resolved to rely only on the power and promise of Yahweh. He is, in a very different way, like the prodigal son who "comes to himself" and returns home to the waiting father (Luke 15:17). In this terse way the narrator suggests there was a change of public orientation.

(iv) Just as judgment follows syncretism, so the entreaty of the king results in a deliverance by the hand of a "savior"-liberator. We are not told who it is nor what he does. At this point the historian is not troubled by such specificity. It is enough to know that when the king trusts himself to Yahweh in public life, there is a safe "homecoming."

The formula in four elements in fact consists in two pairs of assertions. The first pair (vv. 2–3) links *distrust of Yahweh* and *oppression*, i.e., when Yahweh is not utterly trusted, there are negative public ramifications. The second (vv. 4–5) links *turning (repentance) and liberation*, i.e., when Yahweh is genuinely God, there are positive public ramifications. The decision of faith taken by Jehoahaz is the move from the first pair to the second pair, from a posture of *alienation* to a posture of *acknowledgment*. And in making this move the king not only affirms something about Yahweh, that he is truly God. He also affirms something about himself and his public rule, that it is in the arena of Yahweh's sovereign rule, that he acts under the rule of Yahweh. The entire formula makes a primal assertion about the resilient sovereignty of Yahweh and his governance of public history.

Now in preaching such a theological claim as this, some hard intellectual decisions must be made by the preacher (and then by the congregation). Three preliminary comments may be made. First, this is a massive assertion of biblical faith that Yahweh really does order history according to his purposes. Such a view of the historical process refutes attractive, perhaps more compelling alternatives. It rejects the easy assumption of the *autonomy of the nations* to do what they will (see Isa 47). It excludes the seduction of the contemporary notion that "might makes right," or as it is more sanguinely put, "We must negotiate from a position of strength" (see Isa 31:1–3; Zech 4:6). Or it questions the jingoism that the "free West" enjoys some kind of ideological privilege from Yahweh. The way history works, this text claims, is much simpler than all of that. And it may be the task of the preacher to cut through a lot of pseudo-complexity to see that the "mystery of history" has been disclosed to "babes," even if "kings and princes" are slow and resistant in understanding (see Luke 10:21–24). The "mystery" is a "secret" now known by the community of Yahweh. And that secret is what must be proclaimed in every generation. The secret is Yahweh's uncompromising moral governance of public history. The theologian says it here easily. But it could not have been easy then, even in a pre-Enlightenment world.

For us in our time, that view of the historical process is a scandal to our modernity. We know all about human initiative and secondary causes and the interplay of all kinds of social forces. And that is not to be disregarded. So the preacher (and the congregation) must decide about this singular claim of sovereignty in the midst of historical processes. We do not minimize the difficulty in this affirmation. And that difficulty may have something to do with modernity. But that is not the main problem. The main difficulty is in every time, our refusal to face this alternative claim.

Second, the Bible itself knows, as do we, that this simple, rather ideological theory will not cover for all the data. Robert Polzin (*Moses and the Deuteronomist*) has argued that in the book of Judges at least (and undoubtedly here as well) there is an internal struggle in the literature about this moral claim that seems excessively rigid and totalitarian. And many would believe that the poem of Job is also written against such a rigid understanding of God's way of moral accountability.

It takes no great imagination to see that adherence to Yahweh and to Yahweh's claims for justice and freedom do not lead to well-being. Conversely it is clear that resistance to these loyalties does not necessarily lead to oppression. Every totalitarian regime refutes such a claim. Every unanswered act of terror evidences that there is more going on than can be accounted for by this theory.

So the preacher must decide. How much is to be assigned to the theory? How much leeway is to be granted beyond the formula? To hold the theory closely requires "handling" the data to fit the theory. To grant too much beyond is to yield to a modern "failure of nerve" about God's rule in history. The question is not a formal one for the contemporary church. It is a substantive one. What are we to make of the heavy interface between *moral agendas* and the seeming *rawness of power politics*? Shall we be a minority voice holding out for a conviction that once had a consensus and now is an embarrassment? The notion is not marginal for biblical faith.

Third, to the extent that the formulary summary is taken seriously, this is an intensely *theological* matter. It concerns loyalty to this particular God. But the issue is not "religious meaning." Talk about this God is relentlessly *political*. The pay-offs of distrust and loyalty are *oppression and liberation* (saving), utterly political notions. Thus in this view the *highest theological affirmation* is also *sound political policy*. And the reason is that faith in Yahweh is not a "religious" exercise. It is always (since Moses) a decision about public policy. Already in the Exodus the main issue Israel had to face was to decide about the Egyptian empire. Since the Exodus, Israel's faith has been an offer of an alternative public policy which rejects the ways of the empire (Egyptian or any other). In our time with rival ideologies afloat among us, it will take careful and disciplined preaching to make this linkage of theology and politics without being misunderstood concerning pseudo-patriotism.

Note that after the symmetry of the formula in vv. 2–5, this unaccommodating historian adds in v. 6: "Nevertheless." For this moment at least, the high claims of covenant faith are sadly in vain. "Nevertheless," the king proceeded as though none of it were true. The church might ponder the dismal "nevertheless" which shapes so much of our public life, a life seemingly bent on destruction in the false name of security.

But such a response is ineffective here. The sin is too great. The theologian insists on the *moral character* of history with Yahweh.

(b) Jehoash, grandson of Jehu (vv. 10–13) is noted. He is as inconsequential for Israel's faith and history as is James Buchanan in American history. A reflection might be done on the ostensible leaders who have a chance and do not leave a trace of their presence.

(c) Elisha the prophet makes one last appearance (vv. 14–24). It is to be noted that after the anointing of Jehu (9:1–3), the prophets are absent. According to this historian, we have clearly entered a new phase of history. And indeed chapters 12–16 are an in-between period precisely because of the absence of prophets. Where there are no prophets, there is no genuine history. This simple episode is curious here, and perhaps is a fleeting assertion by the historian that the prophets still do govern history. (i) In v. 14, there is a brief reflection on the relation of king and prophet. The mourning of the king shamelessly admits how dependent the king is on the prophet. Thus in a single verse the historian affirms that historical initiative lies with the prophets—and even the king knows it. (ii) Vv. 15–19 report a most curious event, bordering on the magical. The prophet still has non-rational ways of intervening, even in international affairs. The narrative wants to say that administered royal reality is not the source of victory (see Prov 21:30–31). (iii) And the pay-off of the prophetic reprimand is given in vv. 24–25. In v. 19 the prophet chides the king for only making himself three options. The king could have gone all the way to victory, but he stopped too soon. And the result: he defeated Syria three times, but only three times. The narrative leaves the matter inscrutable. But what is clear is that the prophet knows more and can do more than the king can manage or understand. Who knows why an act brings victory or defeat? We would hardly credit such things as the shooting of an arrow. And yet, from Vietnam all the way to the "helicopter mission" in Iran, it is clear that rational, scientific planning is not decisive. If it were, American power would always dominate against lesser force. But it does not. The text affirms what we also know in the dark recesses of our reason. There is more going on than is caught in our public policy. (iv) And just in passing, vv. 20–21 show that the narrative cannot turn loose of its fascination with the man Elisha. He has transformed public life for Israel. He has written large his signature on internal affairs. He has dangerously intervened for the poor. Is it not strange that this massive force in Israel's history occurs on nobody's Sunday School time-line which lists all the kings and maybe misses the history-makers!

Even at death, he is not finished. Albeit perhaps with unbridled imagination, here Elisha is seen to have power even in death. As a dead man, he continues to matter more than many persons ostensibly alive. How odd that this chapter, summarizing the history of northern kings, again turns out to be dominated by this irresistible prophetic presence. It is a signal for how this narrator would have us see all of history. History purports to be about public, identifiable figures. But at its heart, something else operates decisively, well beyond reasonable knowledge, scientific control or conventional expectation. It is not hard to see why the church in its reasonableness has preferred to skip over these narratives. They are too unsettling for our settled minds. We do well to pay attention to that "something else" beyond our capacity and yet embarassingly visible among us.

(3) Amaziah of the south is only two generations removed from the "new beginning" of 842 (14:1–22). But he does not remember much from that newness.

(a) He is presented as appropriately ambiguous, as kings must be in a world of covenant. (i) He does what is right (v. 3). (ii)Yet, he does not (v. 4). He gathered royal power in extreme measure (v. 5), yet he obeyed the torah (v. 6). Caring people in the world must always live in tension between *obedience* and *self-security*. And we say this even as we confess Jesus who was radically obedient and took no effort at self-security (Phil 2:5–11). It is finally Jesus who stands as judge over all our vacillating ambiguity, ancient and modern. How little we have moved from the shrewd ambiguity of Amaziah. Is holding political power in faith an unending juggling act?

(b) Amaziah is a reckless adventurer (vv. 7–14). He had a military success (v. 7). And that may have been his undoing. Heady from victory, he taunted his northern counterpart to battle (v. 8). The response of Jehoash of North Israel is a refusal (vv. 9–10), but it is a baiting refusal. In the scope of three verses, a situation is created which calls for face-saving. And the result is a civil war which leads to a terrible defeat, and the worst of all humiliations, the plundering of the Jerusalem temple. Amaziah is indeed a king who did not count the cost (Luke 14:31–33).

The narrative attests to the extreme and foolish arrogance of Amaziah. It has been conventional to explain this by saying that while the narrative gives no reasons, there are undoubtedly reasons of state behind the personal challenge, perhaps concerning territory or trade or goods. But we may wonder. The military mind feeds itself. The drive for power and control and prestige becomes an end in itself, not a means to an end of the state. National policy and personal inclination together evoke self-serving escalation for no other reason than to "notch the gun" once again. We need only recall the personal posturings of Lyndon Johnson and Richard Nixon in Southeast Asia to know there may be fewer "reasons of state" than there appear to be. So much is personal, desperate need for vindication. The linkage made in the narrative a potent one: foolish politics leads to a raid on the temple. Religious treasures are jeopardized for silly ambitions! How cheaply we trivialize our religion in a game of cock-strutting. Just now one does not know how it will turn out. But we can stand in amazement while Secretary Haig with his brusk arrogance can almost single-handedly reactivate the Cold War with the Soviet Union. Words have a dangerous way to conjure political risk. Perhaps Amaziah like Haig had irresistible public hunger for reassertion. But how costly!

(c) As with his father Jehoash (12:19–20), again there is a conspiracy to death (vv. 17–22). Again no reason is given. The alternate version in 2 Chron 25:27 suggests the reason is disobedience to Yahweh. But that linkage is not given in our text. As he was ambiguous in life, so this king dies a sad death. The general commentary of 2 Chron 25 suggests his military adventurism got out of hand. He unleashed power he could not manage.

(4) Jeroboam (14:23–29) receives passing notice from our narrative. We know his was a long and effective reign. The theologian has a way of bringing great ones to the size of his theological expectation. The one the world applauds becomes a dwarf in the hands of theological criticism. The narrative gives Jeroboam this much credit: He restored the borders of Israel, no small matter. This means he finally overcame the Syrian threat. Under him Israel can again flex its muscle.

But even this is not of the king's doing. It is "according to the promise" (v. 25). History, even royal history, is a way of God's word.

Here as elsewhere the relation of the king to God's promise is ambiguous and problematic. Obviously the king wants to capitalize on everything available from God's promise. Indeed the king wants to take credit himself for whatever good things the promise yields. It is like a public official claiming credit for good weather. No doubt there were royal propagandists (press-officers) who ignored the power of the promise and simply credited the achievement to the king.

But this text is a determined and clear-headed theological statement. This literature is not subservient to royal propaganda. And so the king receives no special credit for the powerful word (promise) of God which has its say in public life, regardless of the crown.

But while the king may want to take credit for the work of the word, the king knows as well that the word is a threat to the royal arrangement. The divine promise is no respector of persons, not even royal persons. It can move against the establishment as much as it can support the establishment. So the king sometimes may welcome the word, but characteristically seeks to silence the promissory word because it will not conform to royal programs.

In this case of Jeroboam, the attempt to silence the divine word is poignantly explicated in Amos 7:10-17. The upfront royal official (the "hatchet-man") in that account is Amaziah the priest. But he is only an agent sent to do the dirty work of Jeroboam (the same one as in our text). In our text (v. 25) Jeroboam is a benefactor of God's active promise. In Amos 7:10, that same effective word is labeled a "conspiracy." The king banishes the prophet and thereby tries to eliminate the free word of Yahweh from his domain. (See the parallel ploy of Jehoiachim later on, Jer 36:20-26.) Jeroboam and Jehoiachim engage in the fantasy that if you can banish the speaker or burn the scroll, you can stop God's overriding intentions. When folks are frightened of the power of God which runs counter to their own purposes and interests, we become prophet-silencers, book-burners, idea-killers, or seizers of printing presses.

But the continuation of the narrative in Amos 7:10-17 makes clear that the resolute word of Yahweh is not so easily nullified. (Indeed that word is never nullified, even in the exile, see Isa 40:8; 55:10-11.) And so Amos, bearer of that word, has his say in vv. 16-17. It is a death-anticipating say, but it is a free say. And the regime is helpless to keep it from being said, or to keep it from coming to reality. In the end, the word is more powerful than the rulers of this age. The preacher might explore how we are all like the king. We do not all wear crowns. But we all preside over our little worlds of self-design. We strongly suspect that the transcendent power which belongs to God (see 2 Cor 4:7) will make a difference. And yet that sure power we want on our side also threatens us because it makes clear we are not in charge. So we both *welcome* the power of God at work in our lives, and

we *seek to limit* it, to keep control of our own act. We are, like this king, strange mixtures of *welcome* and *seeking to limit*.
The preacher might explore:

(i) that profound ambiguity in our lives, i.e., being unable to decide if God is for us or not. Or perhaps trying to decide if we are for God or not.

(ii) that this promissory word is as powerful as Jeroboam found it to be, even against the Syrians. But he also found it to be dangerous, because if we resist it, we are blown away by it. The powerful word as the dangerous word is a useful way to characterize the way Jesus was perceived. See the double statement of Luke 19:47–48. The *people* found him *powerful*. The *leadership* found him *dangerous*.

(iii) that the key issue for most of us is to discern how that promise is at work either to sustain and enhance, or to assault and transform our worlds. The problem is that we cannot have it always one way. It always cuts two ways, like a two-edged sword, cutting both for us and against us.

We observe that in 2 Kings 14:25, the territorial gain made is due to a word spoken by a prophet named Jonah. This is the only mention of Jonah in the historical narrative. As an historical figure, apparently he spoke a word which supported the regime. Of course, we also know about the "book of Jonah" which is likely an ironic, later reflection on the historical prophet Jonah. The relation between the *historical mention* and the *ironic reflection* again points to the ambiguity we have concerning the Word of God. On the one hand, Jonah speaks a promise that enhances Israel. On the other hand, Jonah is a troublesome prophet because he discovers that God is no patron of Israel, but is a free God who does what he wills, is gracious toward whom he chooses (see Exod 33:19), even Nineveh (see Jonah 4:11). The book of Jonah warns kings like Jeroboam and people like us not to presume on the word, not to count unambiguously on the promise, not to assume that we and God's word are natural allies.

All of which points to the hard theological question: Is there a promissory power on the loose in the world that takes actions (healing or judging), which is independent of and not derived from our best efforts? The text presses us to re-decide about God's awesome, healing, dangerous freedom. And the task of the church is not to explain these ancient snippets, but to ask about the dark flow of God's promises, even in our own time.

In vv. 26–27 the theologian offers a crucial comment. Clearly he is little interested in Jeroboam. He will leave that great king for the "secular historians." What preoccupies him is God's deep commitment to Israel, a commitment which endures and which shapes international history. At the center of political history is this compassionate God who will not quit. When there is "none to help," God is moved by the affliction. It has been so since Israel's beginning (Exod 2:23–25). Even in the exile, we are told, God manages the peoples for the sake of Israel (see Isa 43:1–7). If a preacher wants a text for God's compassion with this helpless people, here it is. This is the reason Israel prospers. As we shall see, this poses problems later for the historian. But for now, it is good news. Yahweh alone is Israel's help and keeper (Ps 121:2–8).

Because Yahweh's help is often inscrutable, surprising and not subject to our administration, we incline to hope for and look for other help. We always imagine that help is available from some "lesser god" at less risk. So we are like "Friendly Bob Adams," at the loan company, for "You can always get a little help from a friend." But it is always such little help. Of late we have been much seduced in American culture by the thought that somewhere, someone is available who can fix it, whether an expert, a consultant, a psychologist, the marines.

Well, of course—we can use all the help we can get. But on the whole, the Bible is suspicious of such help and on occasion it is devisive. On the things that really matter, there are no aids which will patch things up. The Bible does not live in a world of "secondary causes." And it does not believe much in "secondary helps." It believes we finally have to face Yahweh as the decisive cause of things, and therefore as the only help. That simple, singular preoccupation with Yahweh is not just because the Bible is "pre-scientific." It is rather because the Bible is quite clear on the fundamental issues. The decision about and response to Yahweh as the principle help in our life cannot be evaded. It is Yahweh, only Yahweh,

who can help (Isa 41:26–28; 43:13; 44:8; 45:5). It is only
Yahweh who gives life and who gives death (Deut 32:39; Isa
45:7). The urgency of this relationship cannot be parceled out
to lesser helps.

A clear and uncompromising statement of this issue is in
the odd narrative of Dan 11. The text describes the destiny of
the faithful under the Hellenistic pressure of the Syrians. In a
sweeping summary of the whole Maccabean crisis, vv. 32–33
anticipate that the faithful torah people will "fall by the
sword and flame, by captivity and plunder, for some days."
They will be persecuted for their faith.

And then the narrative adds a comment in v. 34, drip-
ping with derision. "When they fall, they shall receive a little
help"—damn little! The "little help" will come from the mil-
itary-political effort of the Maccabees. For a while that "liberation movement" will prevail against the Syrians. And
many in Israel regarded this not only as a gain, but as an act
of God. But not the narrator of Daniel. There the "liberation
movement" is dismissed as in fact irrelevant, because it does
not touch the real issue. The real issue, the only issue, is
faithfulness to Yahweh in any circumstance, and the corre-
sponding faithfulness of God toward his people. For this text,
God's faithfulness is so sure that nobody need hope for much
help elsewhere, or imagine either that they will have such
help, or that they will need such help (note the confidence
expressed in Dan 3:16–18). God's own way is enough. It is
indeed "Yahweh alone." Just when there is "none to help"
(see Lam 1:7), this one helps.

Now the preacher is faced not simply with a communication issue, i.e., how to say this. Rather the preacher is faced
with an enormous theological issue. Can this be proclaimed?
Is there such a help when "other helpers fail and comforts
flee"? Is the loyal God yet watching over his own? This text is
unflinching. God stands by. That can be counted on. Nothing
else is so sure. In every generation including our own, the
church has to re-decide its readiness for such a claim. We are
regularly dazzled by "little helps" that seem more available.
But preaching is not the recital of all the "little helps." It is
pointing to an overriding help when none is apparent.

(5) Azariah (elsewhere called Uzziah) reigned 52 years
(15:1-7). Fifty-two years and he gets seven verses! Other

sources indicate he fostered prosperity. 2 Chron 26:6–15 reports his military prowess and administrative leadership. But the key factor is leprosy (v. 5; 2 Chron 26:16–21). In the narrative of Kings, his disease results from religious compromise. In Chronicles it is because of violation of priestly prerogative. Either way, he is a king who does not hold together responsibly political power and religious sensitivity. He is better at *political technique* than he is at honoring the *holiness of God*. Political power is in itself never enough. There runs through biblical faith (perhaps since Gen 3) the foolish notion that enough of power, wealth, knowledge can make one immune to the ways of God (see Jer 9:22–23). The theologian is relentless in his affirmation that worldly power can never be made into an autonomous sphere of activity. And for all our self-impressing secularism, we may observe that this is not simply a modern problem. It has been a problem since the garden scene. Powerful people and powerful societies have always sought immunity from the restrictiveness of Yahwism's abiding moral commitment (see Isa 10:12–14; 47:5–11; Ezek 28:2–10; 29:3–5). The result is some form of leprosy, i.e., of becoming unqualified and unworthy of the trust of power. The Bible offers us the poem of Job for those unconvinced about this stubborn accountability. But our narrative as yet has no doubts on this point. No king, not even Azariah, will outflank the rule of God.

(6) In an important and not very revealing recital, the trivialization and dismal failure of northern politics is reviewed (15:8–31). The point is to show Israel rushing toward destruction. The particulars of the recital need not detain us for long:

(a) Zechariah (vv. 8–12), son of a great king, did evil and was assassinated. The narrator pointedly adds, with his death came the termination of the dynasty, again fulfilling God's dark promise (v. 12; see 10:30). It took only six months for evil to work its way. All of history, even the negativities, is seen as God's way of rule.

(b) After six months of Zechariah, one month of Shallum is enough (vv. 13–15). He is not really a king, but only a barracks pretender. He had idle dreams of power, but no notion of its meaning. He is of no consequence. And yet, argues this theologian, this nobody who knew nothing and only destroys

is an unwitting agent of God. Even the disarray is a working
out of God's purpose which is to bring Israel to ruin. The rule
of God can lead to death, as well as to life. And that of course
contradicts every civil religion.

(c) Conspirators come and conspirators go. Shallum
came easily and now he goes quickly at the hand of
Menahem (vv. 14–22). This latest in the rapid sequence is no
better than Shallum, only he lasts longer—ten years. Beyond
his ability to survive, we may note three things: (i) he was
cruel beyond belief in policy (v. 16; see Amos 1:13); (ii) he
survived by international bribery (19–20). He survived because he was willing to be a puppet of the Assyrians; (iii) in
order to practice as a puppet, he had to raise lots of money
by taxes (v. 20), taking even from the wealthy land-owners.
And that must have evoked enormous hostility. The dismal
recital of Menahem suggests that history-making has become
a sordid royal enterprise in which the king will try any un-
principled thing in order to survive. Completely missing here
is any hint of Israelite memory or covenantal faith. The narrator means to say that when a community forgets the rule of
God, it will surely end. And in the meantime it is reduced to
ignoble strategems like manipulation, conspiracy, bribery,
heavy taxation, and undoubtedly enormous fearfulness.

(d) Pekahiah (vv. 23–26) lasted two years, left scarcely a
track in the sand. History has its incongruities. Menahem by
all odds should have perished, but he dies a peaceful death
(v. 22) and his son pays. Sons do pay for the fantasies of their
fathers, to the third and fourth generations. And this people
in the north has a lot of paying to do. The end of this kinglet
is predictable: more conspiracy.

(e) Yet another—Pekah (vv. 27–31). We are offered one
more nobody, who came by way of conspiracy (v. 25) and left
by the same door (v. 30). He is utterly uncredentialed, so
much 'so that Isaiah (7:9) refuses to name him but refers to
him only as "son of nobody." His fate is like all the others.
Nobodies who rely on self and shrewdness and violence cannot turn the tide of God's death-sentence against this hopeless people. Incidentally we learn of the Assyrian invasion
(vv. 29). *Appeasement* practiced by Menahem did not work.
But *resistance* also did not work. Death is sure.

The narrator rushes through this material, perhaps be-

cause it holds no interest for him, perhaps because it nause-
ates him. The conventional label, "succession of evil kings" is
surely correct. It will not help much to focus on individual
kings. But we must try to get a focus on the whole sorry lot.
The impact is in the sameness of it all: conspiracy-usurpa-
tion-evil-death. What is clear is that public order and public
policy have disintegrated. Public faith has collapsed and
with it public morality. Political chaos and social anarchy
are evident. It is not that "there was no king in Israel" (Judg
21:25). There was an oversupply of pygmies. And the only
thing they have in common is illegitimacy and evil. The theologian scores them not for ineptness or incompetence (which
can be tolerated) but for evil. The theologian believes there is
a moral answerability. Even this sad tale bears witness to
God's sovereignty.

This will be a hard text from which to preach. But perhaps our current time of political disarray, of shifting power
centers, of the imbalance of terror and the collapse of old authorities and trusted conventions, is an appropriate time for
this text. Our nation (and the others) seem to have used up
the supply of visionary leaders who had any large sense of
historical purpose or destiny. And we are reduced to petty
technicians who create, at the most, precarious moments of
stability and equilibrium, but never enough to sustain us or
call us beyond ourselves. When *petty technicians* replace *visionary leaders*, then public life is a series of projections and
images, of doubtful trade-offs and ambiguous phrases which
address no substantive reality.

Such leaders, then and now, reflect the public consciousness. No more significant leadership is possible because the
citizens neither permit, demand nor evoke it. The public consciousness can think of no agenda larger than surviving
through the season. And that becomes a hopeless juggling
act, sure eventually to miscalculate. In that kind of society,
external precariousness is matched by an overriding inanity.

One other factor. Assyria begins to move. The single
super-power is a deep and irresistible threat. In v. 19, Assyria
can be bought off, but only for a while. By v. 29, Assyria is no
longer content with bribes. The empire begins to move. And
it comes with relentless power and savage determination.
Israel may parry but finally is resourceless and helpless. This

theologian sets Israel in a context of political realism. But with this proviso: Assyria and its leader Tiglath-Pileser III (called Pul in v. 19) are not autonomous agents. Assyria is in fact sent by Yahweh (Isa 10:5–10) against Yahweh's people. Thus even imperial moves in the ancient world are confessed to be workings of God's purposes. And that "enemy-God" will not be turned back by armies, by kings, by alliances, by intrigue, or conspiracy. That God will be turned only by the practice of torah ("justice, mercy, faith"; see Matt 23:23). The chronology is complex and obscure. But this much is clear to the theologian. In God's time, in Samaria it is very, very late. The text invites those who come after to see what time it is in the rule of God.

(7) The historian includes a note on Jotham (15:32–38) to make chronological linkages. Jotham is not important, but is a "go-between" of his father Azariah (Uzziah) for whom he was regent (15:5). Again he is given an ambiguous assessment: "he did right . . . nevertheless." However a comparison with his son Ahaz (16:2) indicates they are indeed different. This historian can discern relative differences. We are not in a night so dark that all cats are gray. In this sordid story of national self-destruction, we may be grateful for small gifts of obedience.

(8) This transitional material comes to a desperate end with Ahaz (16:1–20). Things have become hopelessly compromised. As we shall see when we resume the review of Judean kings, we begin with Hezekiah, a good king who makes a new beginning (18:1). But the historian wants us to see the picture whole and will not permit skipping over the sorry parts. So we must linger with Ahaz in whom things are sorry indeed.

(a) The general verdict is massively negative (vv. 1–4). He forgot what it means to be the "Israel of God" (contrast 11:17) and imitated the nations (see Deut 18:9–14). His actions deny the holy rule of God and assume that with enough religious effort, the dynasty and nation can be made safe. Ahaz has yet to learn that such enterprises only breed more insecurity and more anxiety, but never genuine well-being. Ahaz's reign attests to the hopelessness of self-security (see Matt 6:27).

(b) Ahaz, in his frantic drive for security, engaged in appeasement of Assyria (vv. 5–9). His incredible miscalculation mistook the *threat* to be his best *hope*. As is often the case, the enemy comes not by abrasive intrusion, but by a misreading at home. The *destroyer* is perceived as the *savior*. It is in this context that attention should be given to the preaching of Isaiah (Isa 7:1–9). The prophet (see Deut 18:15–22 which contrasts the prophet with the way of the nations) calls the king to faith in Yahweh, both against *fear of little enemies* and *appeasement of the big enemy*. Faith is a "third force" in Israel's politics, according to the prophet. But predictably the possibility of faith is an impossibility to the king who is so enmeshed in his schemes of saving himself. And when that "third force" is rejected, the king is left with only two hopeless alternatives, either *resistance* or *appeasement*.

(c) Then we are given a detailed account of a substitute of an alien altar (and cult) for the altar and cult of faithful Yahwism (vv. 10–20). Fear causes us to do strange things. It skews our vision. It causes us to make wrong identifications. It causes us to abandon oldest loyalties and best judgments for new possibilities which make extravagant promises that cannot be kept. Ahaz's inordinant anxiety caused him to act in "crazy" ways, out of touch with reality as defined by Yahwism. It is the task of prophetic interpretation to distinguish reality from the craziness that passes for reality among frightened, insane people.

Obviously this matter is crucial for this narrative, for the theologian lingers over it in detail. The practice of Yahwism is dismantled. And the old covenant of life (see 11:17) is displaced by a covenant which leads only to death (see Isa 28:15, 18). And all of that is done willingly, not by pressure or coercion from Assyria. Ahaz embraces death, eagerly. At this point, Israel's history with Yahweh should have ended. The policy of Ahaz anticipated the "abomination of desolation" yet to come (see Dan 11:31). What is chronicled here is the change of loyalties which denies the vocation of God's people (see Jer 2:11).

That is an urgent, though awesome preachable point. Is that change at work among us? Is the drive for consumer goods which brackets out public questions of justice like a new altar from Damascus? Is the ideology of the corporate economy which blinds us to the neighbor like a new cult, in which old loyalties seem expendable? We too seem to be at such a place, for the "old God" gives the appearance of being unable to save, and surely irrelevant. It happens in the name of religious legitimacy. But it happens. New gods appear which seem more relevant. And if not relevant, at least more palatable. We do exchange truth for a lie (see Rom 1:25). The theologian puts the issue graphically, perchance that we become aware of what is happening among us. It makes one wonder how late it is. And what the coming exile may hold for us of the old, affluent West.

(9) The final demise of the Northern Kingdom under Hoshea hardly surprises us (17:1–6). It is nearly the predictable outcome. Assyria pushed even harder in its expansionism. But Hoshea, last among the usurpers (see 15:30), again misread the situation. He thought Assyria was the problem, little discerning the real threat or heeding the prophets. This literature insists that Assyria is simply an advance force for Yahweh. The puppet king responded to the visible threat, utterly insensitive to the reason for that threat. He mistakenly thought his history was autonomous, that there was no larger sense, but only a flat interplay of power centers. It never occurred to him (any more than to our contemporary governors) that history has another Referent outside itself. The drama does not change much. Our current rush to militarism in America moves from the same premise that there is only us and we must secure ourselves—utterly oblivious to that other Agent of moral dimension who will not give force its final say.

With that misreading, any stratagem is likely to fail. But the failure came sooner because, even given his crucial miscalculation, Hoshea vacillated. Like a bird frantically flying back and forth (see Hos 7:11), he tried at the same time to bribe Assyria (v. 3) and to join with Egypt in an alliance against Assyria (v. 4). It probably would not have mattered, but playing it both ways predictably ended in trouble.

No great empire will tolerate such double dealing. In *the end* (see Amos 8:2), in the very end, Assyria came to punish a fickle puppet. And the end is exile (already anticipated in Amos 7:16–17): landless, homeless, displaced. Now history with Yahweh has been completely undone. The people promised the land have been ingloriously nullified. All the promises had been kept (see Josh 21:43–45) and how they are negated. A pause for a requiem and a long, long grief.

How can that be preached to Americans who deep in our bones still trust the marines to secure our public life? Perhaps the text could ask—could it happen here? Among us? Perhaps it presses our imagination too much to ask what history is really like. Is it only a power play? Have we only to engage in Kissinger's geo-politics or Cold War or "the China card"? Or are there other moves to make because of a sovereignty well beyond our policies which will never be deciphered but only obeyed? Before that evangelical issue, all our posturings and policy debates pale into insignificance.

The prophets, then and now, soon and late, hinted about torah. But that crucial urging seems so irrelevant in the face of Assyria. It has always seemed irrelevant. It seems irrelevant in our fear and anxiety. It also seems irrelevant when we have "other means." Kings always preside over "other means," even if they are only the tools and means to death. And so it ends in exile. Where else could it end? And one is left to wonder if kings can ever risk hearing prophets. And the wonderment is intense when we know ourselves to be the kings with "other means," kings too anxious to listen, too impressed with our petty alternatives. So the sorry history of human management spends itself and ends in a "land unclean" (Amos 7:17). The issue before us is whether this narrative discernment of history has seen something we have missed.

The Harsh Requirement of Unambiguity
(2 Kings 17:7–41)

Our narrative has at times been that of a reflective theologian and at times that of a discerning historian. And therefore we have referred to the narrator both as historian and theologian. But now the narrator takes a new role, the explicit teacher who does not want the main point missed. The tone here becomes exceedingly didactic. It is not as though this historical recital has been open-ended, inconclusive or ambiguous. The point has been clear enough. And it is important that it not be missed.

But now, in this present chapter, things are more intentional. Here we are at the end of the northern dynasty. It is as though the entire review of the north has been aimed at this single moment of teaching. The conclusions that this historian-theologian now reaches have not emerged in transit, as though the point has only dawned late on the narrator. Rather the entire narrative has been cast to bring us to this moment. And so the didactic move is transparent: *"This was so because . . ."* (v. 7).

(1) The deepest convictions of this narrator-teacher are stated in vv. 7–18. It is a very simple theology: *historical survival as a nation depends on obedience to God's torah*. Disobedience of God's torah, soon or late, will lead to historical disaster. The teaching sounds simplistic, old-fashioned, legalistic, too sure. And, as Job's friends prove, the conviction expressed here can be pressed to absurdity. But for now that is the teaching given us in this part of the Bible. Another text perhaps at another time will have a different ring, but for now we have this one.

The preacher must decide first, not how to preach it (i.e., a problem in *communication*), but if it dare be spoken (i.e., a question of *faith*). This simple theology will not gain much of a hearing in a typical American congregation, especially if this theology be turned upon our own pretensions. All the erosions of rationalism, secularism, scientism, positivism lead us to a notion that history is neutral, waiting for us to give it purpose. And the ultimate purpose given, according to the American modern ethos, is survival, security and affluence. So this text gives us pause. As power shifts among us, as influence wanes, as Western ideology sounds increasingly empty, as we are a shrinking minority in the world, as we find ourselves so often against the forces of liberation in the world, it gives us pause. I submit that this text collides frontally with the main forms of faith operative in our culture, even as I suspect it collided frontally with alternatives in its own time.

The argument of this historian-theologian-teacher here is a negative one. Not that there is prosperity because of obedience, but that there is trouble because of disobedience. So we may ask, what is happening to us? Perhaps this text is premature in the American church where trouble still seems remote. But there are hints of doubt, tremors of lost nerve, dark stirs of unsureness. This teacher is not one-dimensional. He knows the data of history is fluid and admits of different configurations. But he says with moral indignation and impatience: "Can't you see what is happening? Can't you see the connections?" Everything depends on our conviction that God really is Lord, and that his lordship trades in justice. From that lordship, this odd self-understanding comes easily.

(a) A summary of disobedience is given (vv. 7–9a). Israel disobeyed the ultimate command, "No other gods." It did not understand this unique claim, and its own unique identity in history. So Israel imitated the other nations (see 1 Sam 8:5, 20). Israel denied its peculiar character, as people loved by God and defined by God's torah (see Deut 4:6–8).

(b) In vv. 9b–12 particulars are given. These may change from season to season, but whatever form they take, they are denials of God's peculiar place in our life.

(c) There is a call to repentance (v. 13). This teacher is focused on the key role of the prophets who regularly call Israel back to its peculiar way with God among the nations. The prophets are characteristically abrasive and unwelcome. But everything urges them on. The call of the prophets is always, "Repent, turn around, disengage, trust the promises" (see Mark 1:14–15; Luke 3:3; Acts 2:28; 26:20; Rev 3:3, 19). The question of repentance is coming to the American church. And it will not concern the surface matters of sexual morality which are always foremost in civil religion. Rather it has to do with key loyalties that shape public life.

(d) But as sure as this is a call to repentance, there is a refusal to listen (vv. 14–17; see Hos 11:2). To listen is the main demand of Israel's faith (Deut 6:4). To listen means to be addressed and called into being by another who retains initiative. Not to listen is to deny God's rule. Paul Ricoeur asserts that to listen is to admit that we are not self-made. But that of course is the ultimate temptation of God's people then and always. Something happens to "self-made" folks whose ears are incapable of functioning (see Jer 6:10). As a result the category of *obedience* is either dismissed or trivialized.

(e) So the end result of this theology is in the mighty "Therefore" of v. 18a. "Therefore" . . . removal. There are limits to God's patience (compare to Rom 3:25). God has not acted wrathfully or hastily. His action is marked by incredible patience. But there are limits. And that limit has now been reached and transgressed in the shabby history of the north. The preacher must face that hard issue. Of course we know about justification by grace freely given. That is the core of evangelical faith. But in the Bible, that is stated in ways exceedingly dialectical. And where the limit of grace is not faced, free grace likely becomes cheap grace. So the dark side (the "alien work," Isa 28:21) of God's rule must be faced as well. Israel asked with terror, suspecting the answer: "Are you exceedingly angry with us" (Lam 5:20)? The answer is not always the same. But now in this text, the answer is "yes." And that must be faced as a moment of truth in biblical faith.

This heavy saying must not be dismissed as "Old Testament legalism." It is a part of God's way with his people. And this theology must not be preached casually or lightly, lest we trivialize its terror. This teacher understands that God will be taken with utmost seriousness.

(2) In the architecture of this total narrative, this text marks an ending. And yet, it is not the end, for this teacher has yet more to say. In chapters 18–25, the demise of Judah in the south must yet be told. It is a different tale, even if its end is in the same sorry way. And so in this chapter, vv.

18–19a, the text says, "Only Judah." This special case has been anticipated already in 1 Kings 11:12–13, 32, 36. In the midst of the heaviness there is a hope, a very narrow hope, rooted solely in God's promise. But since it is only hope given us, it must not be mocked or disregarded.

(3) In vv. 19b–23 the teacher offers a reprise, so that the main point is not lost. Judah is an exception which leaves a risky way ahead. But that does not change the fundamental claim made here. The main point is exile. The preacher may play with "exile," homelessness. It is a metaphor for much of modernity (see Peter Berger, *The Homeless Mind*). It is a social crisis already seen by Karl Marx. But the exile will not be made complicated by this teacher. He makes a judgment on exile still valid in modernity. *Exile* is linked to disregard of the main claims of *torah*.

(4) In the remainder of the chapter, the teacher (or a subsequent teacher) adds two long reflections which are exceedingly repetitious. In the first of these (vv. 24–28) "counter-exiles" (i.e., the *goyim* sent to Samaria in the place of deported Israelites) do not know the torah they must know to survive. And even the king of Assyria provides for a torah teacher (v. 27). Incredible! It is implausible that this is historical narrative. More likely it is a claim by the tradition that the urgency of the torah is evident even to the nations (see Deut 4:7–8). Nobody can live in God's land without attention to God's torah. The torah implies not only to believing Jews. It is the ground rule for anyone who wants to live a "lion-free" (see v. 26) life in God's creation.

(5) Finally, we are offered a reflective statement on double-mindedness (vv. 29–41). This repetitious statement concerns foreigners who retain old gods and also serve Yahweh. Obviously, the teacher rejects such double-mindedness. Yahweh is never content in such a compromised situation. It will not work because of Yahweh's insistence on our full attention. Nobody can serve two masters (see Matt 6:24), especially if one is intolerant as is Yahweh. But we keep trying. Perhaps this odd text is most closely in tune with our actual religious crisis. For most of us are not bad people, deliberately disobedient. Rather we suffer because of our inability or unwillingness to choose. We flinch from a radical "yes"

which requires saying "no." We do not have enough "purity of heart" to will one thing.

And the result is layer upon layer of fear. We fear God, but we fear most everything else too (see Exod 20:20). Our lives are consumed in fears which admit no resolution. Personally we fear for our being accepted, our competence, our adequate sexuality. And TV commercials trade on that fear of rejection. We fear publicly and so we are mobilized in patterns of fear for new weaponry systems and military adventures. Our lives are beset with paranoia, with sniffing here and there for conspiracy. And finally we are like Solomon in all our glory, utterly anxious (see Matt 6:29).

So the teacher offers a shrewd diagnosis of our situation. We are like the cursed of Lev 26:36 with "faintness of heart," who flee when none pursues, who tremble and run with the flutter of a leaf. The urgency of this entire historical narrative is to decide (see Josh 24:14–15), to embrace a single loyalty and to practice a single obedience. Thus I suggest, what appears in this text to be a flat legalistic reprimand is in fact a shrewd penetration of "the human predicament." The nations take as their normal posture on fundamental matters an ambiguity which resists resolution. Against that, Israel is a people which has decided. It is willed by God to escape the universal weariness of indecision. Israel is called to decide the single question of God and so to live unburdened by fear. Such a people in the ancient world is nearly an unbearable oddity. And such a people in a fearful society at any time is a scandal. But this is the "Israel of God" (Gal 6:16), invited to make a sure, joyous settlement between *its heart* and *its treasure* (Matt 6:21).

The Southern Rush to Death
(2 Kings 18:1—25:30)

These concluding chapters comprise a distinct unit in the presentation of the history of Israel, according to the Deuteronomist. The history of North Israel ended in 721 B.C., as portrayed in 17:7–41. From that point on, this narrative is the simple, uncomplicated story of the southern community, Judah. These eight chapters present Judah's history from 721 until the end of that kingdom in 587 B.C. As is usual in the books of Kings, two things are clear. First, this historian-theologian has *utilized various sources* and gives evidence of them. Second, the portrayal given us is contrived around a *tightly disciplined perspective and set of formulae.*

But neither *sources* nor *formulae* will help the preacher very much. Two other observations may be made which may be more useful. First, it is clear that this historical presentation is shaped to maximize a theological presupposition. That is, the *historical presentation* is used as a vehicle to urge a certain *theological conviction.* That has been true of all this corpus, but it is especially so in this concluding section. On the face of it, that governing theological conviction is that obedience to God's will leads to life, disobedience leads to death. In the first instant, that is indeed the premise of this literature. Of course that is an exceedingly hazardous argument, for it can be heard as the sorriest kind of works righteousness. And along the way, it is clear that not all the data can be forced to serve such a proposal. So it will be the task of the preacher to articulate this theme so that the grandeur and splendor of God's sovereignty becomes apparent and yet properly nuanced.

So I suggest that these texts may be used to help the community reflect on *God's sovereignty* over the nations, and to reflect on *God's providential care* over his faithful community. Such a theme may be acutely relevant in our situation when many conventional supports for public life are shaken and in question. It will not do to make simplistic moves of "relevance" from this text to our time. But it may be a literature which helps us ponder what it means to live in God's world, where God's rule is masked but not voided, where the awesome seriousness of God has its way.

Preaching from these texts need not be an argument about petty moralism which it became among Job's friends. Rather it is to bear witness to the reality of God's sovereignty over public affairs which seem to be without shape or order. What comes clear is that God will not be mocked. Soon or late, God's purposes will score their point.

The narrative is laid out with a simple chronological scheme. I suggest, second, that preaching here may best be organized around the persons of the kings, as models, alternative models of faith and unfaith. It is clear that the text has little or no interest in their persons as such. Rather they are formal figures, almost paradigms of faith. Recently I visited the National Portrait Gallery in London. It is a collection of paintings of Britain's leaders and most prominent persons over the centuries. But they are not photographs. They are portraits, "studies," which means they have been shaped and selected so that the artist and the collection as a whole can make a statement. They are period pieces which embody not only a person but a time and a perspective.

That is what we have most clearly in this last portion of our literature. The preacher may take the task to study the portrait, to find out what statement is being made by this portrait painter of a theologian. I suggest that taken in a series, these seven kings considered here would make a Lenten series, for they offer a "passion narrative," as Judah moves closer to its death. Each king along the way contributes to the shape of that death in Jerusalem. In a way, these kings are "stations of the cross," as the people of David make their way to their suffering and death.

The seven kings in eight chapters need to be seen as a whole, even though a sermon might be done on each. Each king is to be seen in the presence of the others, moving from the new beginning after 721 to the dismal, desperate approach of 587. This movement must have been a source of fascination as well as dismay to Judah. They asked how and why it happened. It will be important that these texts not be handled as "reportage." That is not what they are. They never were intended so and surely are not now. Portraits are not created to portray dead, one dimensional memories. Rather

they are to make a statement which may be skewed and over-
stated, but always with dimensions of depth and ambiguity.
Such a collection of portraits may enable us to consider our
life (both personal and public) afresh. Where is it going? Why
is it turning as it does? Are we committed to courses of action
which spell our doom? Or can't it happen here, to us? What
is the nature of historical freedom? Are we fated? The evidence is not all given. But the portraits permit and preclude
some interpretations. The text invites us to study the portraits to discover they make a statement not only about
then—but about now.

Hezekiah—Faith with a Last Quick Sell-out (18–20)

The tradition is especially fascinated with Hezekiah, and
gives extra coverage to his reign. The historical data on this
great king is complicated for two reasons. First, it gives us
pause that the same narrative, with only slight change, appears in Isaiah 36–39. And we must ask why that is so. Second, the actual historical events behind the text concerning
the Assyrian invasion are obscure and difficult. But our concern now is the text as we have it, even though it requires
that we ignore some widely recognized problems. This much
we know. Hezekiah had a long reign, played a daring game of
diplomacy with his various neighbors, especially Assyria. He
is best known for his closeness to the prophet Isaiah, and for
the unexpected deliverance of Jerusalem in 701. The text of 2
Kings 18–20 seems to include duplication and repetition and
it is hopeless to sort out those historical matters.

A. Hezekiah is presented in 18:1–37 as a model man of
faith. The preaching potential here may go in two directions.
On the one hand, Hezekiah is a pure model, nearly too good
to be true. But this text believes such utter faith is a human
possibility. On the other hand, the text is candid, showing
that even such a man of faith wavers and doubts. Faith is
never a settled state, but is always a fresh battle, facing new
temptations and requiring new decisions.

(1) In 18:1–18 there is a tension of theology and reality.
This text permits the preacher to focus on this question: Is
faith possible? What does it cost? What are the risks? What
are the results of such faith? Such an issue lets Hezekiah ap-

proach the questions both of Abraham and of Job. On the one hand, Abraham is the faith-father who fought for that "impossible possibility." On the other hand, Job is that titanic man who discovered that faith is disinterested and does not produce a gain.

(a) Vv. 1–8 presents a simple picture of a man of uncomplicated faith. Hezekiah is cited in v. 3 as the most faithful king since David. V. 5 goes even further to say there was none like him before or after. The positive side of Hezekiah is presented in v. 5. *He trusted*. The term is *batah* and we will return to it. He relied completely on Yahweh's capacity to work goodness for him. This governing verb is followed by two other favorite words of this tradition, he *held fast* to Yahweh and he *kept* the commandment. He trusted perfectly and it impacted every aspect of his life. The upshot is that he was obedient. There is no well-intentioned or romantic faithfulness that does not engage in concrete obedience. Thus any split between works and faith is impossible here.

The concrete action Hezekiah took was to remove all symbols of distrust and disobedience (v. 4). Now it is likely that among us there are not such obvious and brazen symbols of distrust and disobedience, for this presentation is highly stylized. But the faithful community can focus on the way of undivided faith and the symbols of unsure and compromising loyalty. Those symbols must be removed and eliminated. There is no space here for a *passionate confession* combined with *slovenly social practice*. The text presents a nice combination of *perfect trust and radical obedience*, i.e., "trust and obey."

That pure faith on the part of Hezekiah yields two results. One, it leads to well-being (v. 7). Hezekiah's reign is remembered as a time of prosperity (see the extravagant claims of 2 Chron 32:27–30). Two, the king had power to act for the liberation of his people (vv. 7–8). Now such a statement can be read in several ways, perhaps as a call to war or as a crusade of fanaticism. Rather, I suggest, the text holds a unified view of life. There is close linkage between right faith, just economics and political freedom. And where there is not faith, there will not be prosperity or freedom. Hezekiah's faith made liberation possible.

(b) In vv. 9–18 the text adds two other notes. First, in vv.

9–12, there is offered a counter model of the northern kingdom, rival of Jerusalem. Here the symmetry is equally clear
and right. Only now it is negative. In v. 12, the north has not
listened. In v. 11, and as a result, there is exile. Disobedience
leads to displacement. Disregard of torah leads to drastic dis-
orientation and disorder. As a perfect foil to vv. 1–8, the same
point is made. God's will, embodied in the torah, is the only
source of well-being. This is a rather odd placement of this
report, but it serves to enhance the model of Hezekiah as an
embodiment of faith.

Second, in vv. 13–18, the text backs away from the
grand claims of vv. 1–8. Here it gives Hezekiah some historical reality. He did not believe utterly in Yahweh. He did
not ignore political reality. So these verses tell about appeasement and accommodation. Hezekiah is no story-book
"knight of faith." He counts costs and accommodates as is
necessary. Preaching from this text should not lead to con-
doning accommodation. But it may permit a subtle and
sensitive portrayal of the countless little ways in which the
grand resolve of vv. 1–8 is domesticated. We live between
the grand celebration of vv. 1–8, and *the guarded candor* of
vv. 13–18. And what is at issue for Hezekiah and every person of faith is the will of God: there shall be no other loyalties, no other accommodations, alliances, appeasements.
But life, even for Hezekiah, is more daily than that. And we
are burdened with anxiety. Hezekiah may be *a model*. But
he is also *a question*. Is it possible to have no other loyalties? The preacher cannot answer for the congregation. And
in any case an answer should not be given soon. But the
text makes it an unavoidable question. Preaching here may
help folks know it is one of the unavoidable questions of our
lives.

(2) In vv. 19–27 we are shifted into a world of bold challenge. The enemy, the voice of accommodation, the power of
anxiety and fear, does its work. In the speech of the Assyrian
agent we have an echo of the voice of the serpent in the garden (Gen 3:1–5) and an anticipation of the voice faced by
Jesus concerning his vocation (Matt 4:1–11). It is a persistent
voice which tries to talk folks out of radical faithfulness. The
faith of Hezekiah, like our own faith, is under assault from
the enemy which can always suggest an easier way. The
preacher is invited to a grand scene of public diplomacy. The

preaching task is to translate that into the countless daily ways that the voices of the empire have their assaulting say. Faith is daily under attack and erosion. The assault is dangerous because the alternatives proposed seem stronger, more attractive, more satisfying. In such a busy scene of competing loyalties, the deepness of faith may seem modest, quiet, defenseless, perhaps driven from the field.

The main action here is in the speeches by *the voice of the empire* who is the enemy of faith, the enemy of the torah. The empire is not just a political or military threat, but the voice of self-sufficiency (see Isa 10:13–14). It offers an alternative principle of reality. And the narrative moves even this great king Hezekiah to the brink of concession. The faithful are always at the brink of selling out. Like the snake, the speaker means to challenge the authority of God, to doubt God's promises, to compromise God's lordship, to create a situation in which God need not be taken with such singular seriousness. And that is the preachable point: must God be taken seriously? Can God be taken seriously? What are the alternatives? And what would it mean to take God seriously in the face of an imperial serpent? The speeches of challenge and seduction are in vv. 19–25 and vv. 27–35, interrupted only by the feeble appeal of v. 26. The drama of *massive confrontation* and *feeble protest* anticipate the whirlwind of God and Job's feeble, innocuous response (Job 40:3–5, 42:1–6). Only in our text the seduction comes armed with tanks and missiles.

I suggest a sermon (or three sermons) might follow the main rhetorical moves of the text.

(a) The first of these (vv. 19–25) is a play on the word "trust" *(batah)*, already used once in v. 5. Hezekiah *trusts*. Now that trust is brought under close scrutiny. The Assyrian diplomat means to break Hezekiah away from his God, to make the king vulnerable to the threat and seduction of the empire. In v. 19 the basic issue is put. Whom do you trust? Words and nice religious slogans will not do. Neither will mere patriotic jingles. Nor can you look to a political ally, for the allies are weak and fickle (v. 21). Nor can you finally rely on the God of Israel (v. 22), for against the empire Yahweh the God of Israel is a feeble alternative. The preacher and the congregation should not flinch. It is the truth. Against the attractive options of the day, military might, political power, psychological sensitivity, more goodness—the God of the

Bible is not very compelling. God is one before whom we are embarrassed (see Isa 53:2–3). In the context of civil society this God is foolish against all the wise, weak against all the strong (1 Cor. 1:18–25).

And besides all of that, says the voice of the imperial snake, God sent me. This is not against God, but on behalf of God. So on what ground could we resist the great Assyrian claim?

(b) The second rhetorical move is made by the "great king" (v. 28) and runs through v. 32. For starters, we might ask if this is irony. Is the Assyrian the "great king"? Is he the "great one" as was Herod or Caesar or Death? We can't tell if this is just a formal title or a bit of sarcasm. But for vv. 28–32, he is the real one. He does all the talking. This "father of Assyria" "knows best," better than Hezekiah or Yahweh or the torah. It is so like the parent chiding a little child, excluding silly possibilities:

> Do not be deceived (v. 29).
> Do not let Hezekiah make you trust (v. 30)
>   (again that word "trust").
> Do not listen to Hezekiah (v. 31).
> Do not listen to Hezekiah (v. 32).

The rival claims are sharply delineated. Israel believes the Lord will deliver. Against that, Assyria offers an alternative peace of "grain, wine, bread, vineyards, olives and honey," but in a foreign land (vv. 31–32).

On this folks need help. We may imagine we do not usually have issues drawn so clearly as were these. But they are never that clear until someone with a clear tongue speaks it clearly. The people of God is called to distinguish between the claims of Yahweh and the voices around us trying to talk us out of our faith. We are all tempted to quit listening, to turn our ears to more attractive voices.

(c) The third rhetorical move is in vv. 33–35. It is a series of rhetorical questions. They are questions that do not wait for an answer. They assume the answer is perfectly obvious and none needs to verbalize it. The implied conclusion to this question is:

> No god of recent memory has delivered.
> The gods of Hamath and Arpad are eliminated.

The gods of Sepharvaim, Hena and Ivvah are absent.
The god of Samaria has failed.
Consider—Yahweh is like all the others. Judah has no more
hope than the other hopeless peoples. They failed, so will this
one. Here is the end of religion, unable to withstand the reason and power of the empire. The end of religion and the
questions of this text remain for the church. Is there anything
distinctive here? Is our faith just like all the others? Is there a
resource here which permits an answer?

And there the matter is left. The king offers no refutation
(vv. 36–37). He has only the good sense not to answer too
quickly. Preaching in these texts may alert the church to our
proper faith situation. Faith is on the defensive. It is under
assault. And we are feeble in making answer, not because we
are cowards or unsure, but because the erosion is effective.
Hezekiah is a man of faith. But he must have wondered how
long it made sense to resist Assyria. Assyrian promises not
only sounded good. There was evidence of a fulfillment. The
issue before us now is not America versus Russia or capitalism versus communism. It is the gospel against every com-
prehensive alternative. And in our daily life, it is the gospel
against every form of self-help, every offer of security. So far
in this text, only the question is put. The preacher (along
with the congregation) must await an answer.

B. Now for the first time in this narrative (19:1–27) the
prophet appears. Indeed, it is likely that chapter 18 is staged,
as it now is, to create a context for the prophet in chapter 19.
As a result, this chapter has a new kind of dialogue. In 18 the
exchange is between the *stridency of the empire* (vv. 19–25,
28–35) and the *feebleness of Israel* (vv. 26–27, 36–37). Now it
is between *the uncertainty of the king* and *the assurance of the
prophet*. The preaching issues are to engage the congregation
on both sides of that dialogue, both to embrace the *uncertainty* as our own, and to assert the *sureness* of the prophet as
also belonging to us in the household of faith. We are both
faithful and fickle, both doubters and believers. This text requires us to live on both sides of that issue (see Mark 9:24).

(1) In 19:1–13 our attention is on the interaction of king
and prophet (vv. 1–7). (The resumed speech of Assyria in vv.
8–13 adds nothing new.)

(a) King Hezekiah is pictured as a man of faith at the

brink of dismay. He behaves like a desperate believer. He
goes to church. He puts on religious clothes of sorrow. But he
believes more than that. He summons the prophet (v. 2). He
does not believe his religion is a closed system. He allows for
a new word to be spoken.

But beyond that, Hezekiah is a king and a man of faith
who can still spot the real issue when it appears. He does not
know what may come of it. But he does see the main point.
God has been mocked. God's word has been despised. God's
rule has been trivialized. It is a question about the profana-
tion of life. How far can the cheapening of life go unanswered? Are there boundaries beyond which ruthless
terrorizing by the powerful cannot be done? Hezekiah has a
hint and a hope. His hint is much less firm than is Paul (Gal
6:7).

But the hint has a firm basis. The reason God is not
mocked is because this is *a living God.* This is a God who does
his own thing, not one who is only an echo of Israel, not a
conjuring of the prophet, not a figment of royal imagination.
God is not mocked, because in reality God is God. The Assyrian king has not noted that decisive difference from all the
other gods. He assumed this God was like the others who
were only shadows (vv. 33–35). But Hezekiah, model of faith,
locates the issue and knows its resolution.

(b) And the response of the prophet confirms Hezekiah's
hope: *Do not fear!* That is the fundamental speech of the prophetic tradition of Isaiah (see 41:10, 13, 14; 43:1; 44:2). It is
not casual speech but it is the most sovereign word God has
to place in the ears of his covenanted subjects. Hezekiah has
a hunch that God will be God. Isaiah offers a strident assertion that in this, as in any circumstance, the power alien to
God can scare, threaten, intimidate and seduce. But finally
that power cannot have its way against the living God. The
prophetic response to the king is not peripheral. It is definitional. The king must hear such a prophetic voice. It is the
very speech of the prophet that gives faith back to the king.
And we are always frightened kings waiting to be addressed,
having our faith-hunches and hopes grounded in bouyant reality (see Rom 10:14–15).

(2) The exchange between king and prophet, between
hint and sureness, is intensified in vv. 14–28. Now the inter-

action is between prayer and oracle, between request and
response.

(a) The prayer of the king (vv. 14–19) is a stylized prayer
of lament. It is a model of evangelical faith. The prayer begins and ends with Israel's most fundamental affirmation:
"Yahweh alone is God" (vv. 15, 19). That is not a conclusion
reached in prayer. It is a premise of Hezekiah's prayer. Israel
knows in its prayer life that it prays to this God who is the
only true God. In this act of prayer, Hezekiah distances himself from the Assyrian miscalculation. The Assyrians thought
all gods were alike and none really mattered in the world of
power. But true prayer depends on this premise, even if it
strikes imperial rationality as silly or scandalous.

The prayer employs four imperatives which ask God to
attend to this dangerous situation of helplessness. The first
three verbs in v. 16 are reminiscent of Exod 2:23–25 where
Israel's faith begins: "incline, open, hear." Israel is bold to
assert that this God is attentive to its helplessness and hopelessness. This prayer is offered when "other helpers fail and
comforts flee." This God is indeed the "help of the helpless."
The fourth imperative in v. 19 comes to the main point:
"Save"—rescue, deliver, liberate. It is the cry "Hosanna"
(Mark 11:9) which in fact means, "Save, I pray." In the tri-
umphal entry of Jesus, the ones who have no help turn to this
one. This prayer knows that there is one who can invert the
situation because Assyria is not really in charge.

The center of the prayer then is in v. 16, a theme already
sounded in v. 4. There is *mockery of the living God*. Vv. 17–18
provide evidence for this accusation against Assyria. The premise of the prayer is that this God will be pushed only so far
before God acts in the interest of holy sovereignty. And Assyria, in its ruthless cynicism, has crossed the line and will be
punished.

This text, like the preaching to which it calls us, is an
absurdity, if the world is to be judged by visible power arrangements. But this prayer and our use of it make assertions
against visible power arrangements. Hezekiah is bold to pray
because he counts on that other political reality that Assyria
inevitably has not noted. And that is the question always
before the church—if we believe in, trust in, rely on this other
One.

(b) Hezekiah does not wait long. Immediately (as the text presents it) there is a prophetic oracle answering the prayer and setting Assyria in a new context which it cannot resist (vv. 21–28). The oracle *recontextualizes* the world of Assyria. Assyria had assumed it was alone in the world. The oracle is not addressed to Hezekiah or to Israel, though their futures are given in it.

The poem is in four parts:

(i) Vv. 21–23a. The prophet returns to Hezekiah's theme of "mock" in vv. 4, 16. Isaiah is as sure as Paul (Gal. 6:7): God is not mocked! And to make the point, *the unmocked* one is named with majestic splendor: The Holy One of Israel. Yahweh is the unutterable one who stands with Israel (see Josh 1:9). Assyria has committed a gross miscalculation, not reckoning with Yahweh's overwhelmingness.

(ii) Vv. 23b–24 articulates the pride of Assyria which is a ludicrous self-assertion. Note the repeated "I, I, I, I, I. . . ." Hezekiah, on behalf of Israel, had found life by saying "Thou" to God (vv. 15, 19). But Assyria can say only "I," never "thou." And so Assyria, for that wrong reference, comes to death.

Israel's prophets frequently indict Israel or a foreign nation by putting words in their mouths. Here, in vv. 23–24, the statement attributed to Assyrian ambassadors is a way of "mocking" Yahweh. The primal claim of Assyria here is *autonomy*, i.e., the notion that the empire is not accountable to any God, to any moral principle, to any transcendent purpose. So the policy of Assyria is presented in the form of public shamelessness (see Jer 8:12: "No, they were not at all ashamed; they did not know how to blush").

The statement in the mouth of the Assyrians is a boast about technology, in which all value questions have been screened out. The empire is accused of doing everything of which it is capable, in the interest of security, and one suspects, in the interest of self-aggrandisement. The main claims for this self-securing technology in v. 23 are not even addressed to political assertion but to scientific competence. The statement celebrates the capacity to capture the secrets of the creation. Only in v. 24 is a move made concerning the political realities. The statement presents Assyrian imperial expansion extending as far as Egypt itself (see Nahum 3:8).

The empire had overstepped itself in its unbridled greediness. Too late the public question is raised: How much is enough?

The poetic capacity to put this statement in the mouth of the enemy suggests an artistic sensitivity which may be useful in preaching. First, the form of expression makes this statement: actions speak louder than words. The empire is saying things it does not know it is saying and does not mean to say. This is a point worth raising, given the self-serving way of our culture. What in fact is being said by our policies and our budgets? Are we making announcements that we do not know we are making? Would a visitor from another planet see some things about us that we do not see about ourselves? What are we so frightened of? And if we are so frightened, does it mean we do not really have any faith? Is our self-securing really out of a suspicion that God does not govern history and order the nations?

Second, the preacher might treat this interaction of Israel-empire-prophet as a drama in which the contemporary community considers itself in all the roles. Specifically we are accustomed to think of ourselves as Israel, or in this case, the besieged king. But perhaps we are in fact cast in the role of Assyria. We are not the people who protest against the mocking of God, but we are the God-mockers. Then one might ask about the ways in which God is mocked in our public life, and what the costs of that will be.

Perhaps this passage can usefully be linked to two passages usually dated somewhat later. First, as a foil against such imperial self-assertion, see the counter assertion of Yahweh in Isa 44:24–28 which has a long series of self-announcements:

who says . . .
who says . . .
who says . . .

But it is claimed, unlike the imperial pretender, this voice has the power to do what he speaks:

I have spoken and I will bring it to pass;
I have purposed, and I will do it (Isa 46:11).

The capacity to mean what he says and do what he says is as old in Israel as the memories of the Hexateuch. Thus see Josh

21:43–45: "Not one of all the good words which the Lord has
spoken to the house of Israel had failed. All came to pass."
Thus the claim of Yahweh in Isa 44:24–28 is juxtaposed with
the claim of Assyria in our passage. The difference is that Assyria cannot do what it says, because it is not god, not a voice
of genuine authority, as is Yahweh.

And more directly, Job 28:1–11 characterizes the royal,
scientific exercise of probing the mysteries of creation. The
claims made there are closely paralleled to those in our text.
But then Job 28:12 asks after all of that, "But where shall
wisdom be found?" That is, none of the foregoing shows wisdom. It shows technology, but it does not evidence wisdom
which pays attention to the overriding and unyielding purposes of Yahweh. None of this mighty exploitative investiga-
tion (e.g., the ability to find off-shore oil, the capacity to
explore space, the ingenuity to mount new weapon systems)
shows a real understanding of life in Yahweh's world. And
therefore all of the scientific capacity of the empire is futile
without the central recognition and embrace of Yahweh's
rule, which requires torah obedience. And of course the indictment made of the empire is rather like Catch-22, for the
empire cannot concede the lordship of Yahweh without in
fact ceasing to be the pretentious empire it is.

So I suggest that a preachable point is to make clear precisely that dilemma of Catch-22, not for ancient Assyria, but
for our own situation. For the truth is that in public life, we
are "mockers of God." And the further inescapable truth is
that we cannot genuinely heed the command of the true God
without giving up all of the pretentions which as of now supply the nerve for the empire.

This accusation which mocks (i.e., it mocks the mocker)
is the centerpiece of this poem which is developed in a most
effective way. This anti-mocking in the form of mocking is
bounded in v. 22 and in v. 25 with questions. The first is an
accusation. The second is a counter assertion of Yahweh
which then proceeds to assert a lordship to which Assyria
falsely aspires.

(iii) In vv. 25–26, Yahweh takes credit for Assyria's imperial successes (see Isa 10:5–6). Even in its prosperity it was
not Assyria's own doing, but Yahweh had decreed it. The
prophet boldly assigns all imperial success to Yahweh.

(iv) In vv. 27–28 Yahweh withdraws support from Assyria (see Isa 10:15–19). The implication is that without Yahweh's support, Assyria—with all its arms and resources—cannot survive and prosper. The prophet makes an audacious claim. Assyria is as dependent on Yahweh as are Hezekiah and Israel. The Holy One of Israel is also the Holy One of Assyria. There is no other (see Isa 19:24–25).

The response of the poet correlates with the prayer of the king. Hezekiah had dared to believe Yahweh rules the affairs of the nations. Now it is affirmed. In the prophetic response Israel is rather incidental. Assyria is subject to Yahweh and is addressed by Yahweh. And that is true even when Assyria disregards that sovereign address.

The poem concludes with a recital of "I" statements on the part of Yahweh. So there is a deliberate contrast of Assyria's self-proclamation and Yahweh's self-proclamation. Hezekiah is a helpful fugure for us in this context. It is now a contest between Yahweh the God who is promise-maker and promise-keeper, and the empire which values nothing human. The situation of the contemporary believer before the live word of God is like the situation of Hezekiah, placed precisely and desperately between two voices and two rival claims. But in this instant (though not everywhere, as we shall see) Hezekiah is a model of faith. He takes the "right" side. He prays to Yahweh, against the mockers.

Now the preacher must attend to a very real problem. We are inclined always to imagine that had we lived then, the choices would have been clear. The choice between the two claimants of loyalty is apparent. But it is not that apparent, certainly not now. But in fact it was not then either. It became apparent only as the prophet-poet had the courage to lay out the issue, to overstate and simplify and dramatize so that the choice could be discerned. The people who listen to the preacher today live in a context of wickedness. But as much as anything, we live in a context of unclarity and ambiguity. Preaching from the text requires not simply articulating the old choice. It requires as best as we can articulating the present choice between the self-serving of the system (perhaps "the American system") and the choice of Yahweh. And we are hard pressed to know what that choice is. But we know this much. It means a break with the self-serving of the empire. And it means attending to the devalued ones whom the empire discounts, but who this other holy king values inordinately (see Luke 7:34).

I do not suggest a frontal attack on the American system of imperialism, for that is both too difficult, and too easy. Therefore the preacher need not offer a simplistic analysis. It is enough to let the text have contemporaneity, to know that power as a temptation to self-aggrandisement is forever present. But the account is not just a political critique. It dares to say that such self-serving is a theological issue, because Yahweh is the one who sides with the needful. Thus Hezekiah's prayer is not that of a buoyant king, but of a desperate man. And there is something dramatically powerful in the contrast between this desperate king "who has no clothes" and the strident empire which is well dressed, but on the way to death (compare Isa 47).

(c) The remainder of the chapter (vv. 29–37) is only an aftermath of assurance. In vv. 29–31, a sign of promise is given. But it is no visible sign. It is a promissory word: In three years, Jerusalem will be safe. In vv. 32–34 there is a specific protective promise for Jerusalem. And finally in vv. 35–37 there is historical actualization. Jerusalem is in fact saved against the enormous odds of the empire.

At one level, one may engage in marvel over that miraculous deliverance. But that is not really our issue. I suggest two other issues more pertinent. First, the congregation might be invited to explore the metaphor of Assyria. Who is Assyria today? Perhaps Russia—or perhaps America? Or perhaps the bully on the playground or in the office. Assyria is wherever some use power to exploit and terrorize others.

Second, the real issue is a battle for God. Is God only a projection of the way the world is organized? Or is God an effective agent who has his own way and his own plans and hopes that are done by his zeal (v. 31)? The reality of God is the deep question of our lives. It is a very old question, but peculiarly urgent now. And the preacher must know that the issue will be settled by faithful speech, by responsive assurance, by the defense of the mocked one (see Matt 27:29; Acts 17:32), by saying boldly, "Do not fear" in a world mad with fear. It is always the dead one come alive (vv. 4, 16) to whom witness is yet to be born (Acts 2:32).

C. Judah is never far from Assyria in these years, never beyond fear of and wonderment about the empire. But in this chapter (20:1–21) there is a focus on the person of the king. There is some vacillation between the person of Hezekiah and the public office of the king.

(1) In vv. 1–11, the issue is the healing of the king. He is near to death. The prophet warns him of death to come (v. 1).

(a) The king prays (v. 3). This is not a prayer of penitence or remorse. It is a prayer of healthy self-assertion. Surely he has not been "good and upright" for nothing. The prayer is close to bargaining, very much as Job might have prayed. But good prayer must always be at the brink of bargaining, if it is to avoid conventional submission and phoney humility.

(b) The prayer yields results! The prophetic response (vv. 4–7) is that God will heal his faithful servant. This exchange is unlike that of Job. In Job such virtue and fidelity yield nothing. But here the king makes his claim good. The response of God to the king is more like his response to enslaved Israel in Exod 2:23–25:

> I have heard your prayer,
> I have seen your tears,
> I will heal you.

The healing includes medicinal action in v. 7, but interestingly, the *healing* is linked to *deliverance* (as in Exod 15:26 where the great deliverance ends, "I am your healer"). One of the incidental gains here is to overcome any split between *personal well-being* and *public transformation*. They come together. So the God who heals the king is the one who rescues the city. And any king who wants *personal healing* without *saved city* is a failure (more on this later).

(c) Asking for a sign is paralleled to that of 19:29–31. But here it is a staggering sign. It is a manipulation of the sun on the sun dial. There is no natural way to explain what is stated here. It is a marvel intentionally paralleled to that of Josh 10:12–13. It is an assertion that the lord of the heavens mobilizes his creation for the well-being of his people. Care must be taken not to trivialize the report nor to mock God by giving an explanation. It is only stated, not proved or explained or made credible. The healing of the king and the rescue of a city are interventions that transgress the expectations of royal reason.

(2) After that remarkable inversion, vv. 12–21 come as a disappointment. Hezekiah had prayed twice, once for himself (20:3) and once against Assyria (19:15–19). Each time he was answered by God through the prophet (19:20–28; 20:4–7). That should have left him deeply assured and secure.

But the appeasing tendency noted in 18:13–18 is his ultimate reaction to political danger. Even this healed man of faith is less than fully faithful. Even he hedges his bets. The line has been clearly drawn by the prophet against the Assyrian danger. But the king will not leave it there. He negotiates with the enemy. He discloses state secrets. He shares family treasures. He makes an alliance with the very mockers of the living God (v. 13).

And why? Perhaps the narrative oversimplifies. But the narrator has a proposal (v. 19). Hezekiah did this act of treason against his God and against his own state because he takes a very short-term view of life, abandoning the future generation, looking only to his own comfort and safety until he dies. And by the end of the narrative, Yahweh seems forgotten. Assyria at the last has its day. For now Assyria has won out, by the complicity of this most faithful of Judean kings. Earlier we saw that the king prayed not only for personal healing, but also for rescue of the city. Now he has forgotten the city and looks only for his own immediate interests.

In the parallel in the book of Isaiah, this narrative of guilt and betrayal is set just before the great poetry of the exile (Isa 40) and following. It is as though this self-indulgent policy of Hezekiah has brought his whole people to the dark night of exile. And in the end, Judah is as north Israel (2 Kings 18:11) and for the same reason. They did not trust Yahweh. In the shape of the book Isaiah, this is the trigger for exile. In the book of 2 Kings, the tale takes another century to unfold. But the outcome is the same.

In preaching on this, it may not be wisest to deal with international politics. That may be so, first, because parallels are not easily drawn and we must not be reductionist. Second, most of us are not Secretaries of State. The real issue is not coping with a hostile imperial power. The deep and urgent issue is faith in a world that offers a hundred alternatives, some seductive, some intimidating, all attractive, against a God who seems less than sovereign. The issue is not how marginal faith is to politics. It is rather how crucial faith is to the very shape of our life.

So the congregation may be invited to face the many moods and seasons of Hezekiah—model of faith, compromise, boldness in prayer, fear in sickness, delivered, yet an appeaser. So is the brooding of faith with us all. We live always before the taunting empire, sometimes happily with a sure prophet, sometimes willing to sell our children for a moment of peace. The text claims that in all these changing seasons, there still moves the zealous one who lives and will not be mocked. If not mocked, then Paul's urging may hold: "let us not grow wearing in well-doing . . . do not lose heart" (Gal 6:9).

With 20:19, we reach the dramatic end of the reign of Hezekiah. It is a dismal, disappointing end, an act of pragmatic cowardice when we had expected more from this man of prayer and piety. Indeed, it is an end that is unworthy of the man Hezekiah, as the theologian has portrayed him. That dramatic end in itself is enough for reflection.

But the preacher may also reflect on how this ending is variously handled in the tradition. There is no doubt that this is such a sell-out that it causes us to gasp. And surely the tradition intends us to lose our breath here. The editorial comment in vv. 20–21 is a marvel of understatement. It is as though the main point is made. This theologian has not the will or imagination or interest to go further. Perhaps after such an ignoble act, the theologian cannot bring himself to pay attention. He may be disappointed in his own major character! It is as though the theologian is saying to the reader—"Think about it!" Think about such a pragmatic, short-term sell-out. Think about playing footsie with worldly power for a moment of peace.

But this abrupt ending may be carried in an even more dramatic direction. The preacher may steal a glance at the parallel account in Isa 39. The text thus far is the same. The conclusion is the same sorry spectacle of a king so turned in on himself and his immediate well-being that he forgets the demands of his office. (Hezekiah needed a Joab to goad him into being a king and not just a self-pitying man (see 2 Sam 19:5-8). In the Isaiah version, we arrive at the same caesura in the structure of the literature. And that break in the literature means to articulate a discontinuity in the historical process. Note that in the tradition of Isaiah, there is a long pause before the next words in Isaiah 40. As is well known, chapter 40 begins "Second Isaiah" in the exile two hundred years later. So how long is the break between 39 and 40? As long as from the eighth century to the sixth century. As long as from the failure of Hezekiah to the rise of Cyrus (see Isa 45:1). As long as it takes the gospel to move from hopelessness to comfort. For Jews and for Christians, the space between is as light years, for the time between witnesses the destruction of Jerusalem, temple and monarchy. Indeed, in Isaiah 40, we are a very long way from chapter 39, no matter by what measure.

The narrative of 2 Kings takes us more immediately to the next episode than does the parallel of Isaiah which skips over things. For the book of Isaiah, the break is presented more decisively and more radically. But note how the continuity is carried in 2 Kings. The next element in the story is not much, only Manasseh, only the king who is the immediate cause of the end. It is as though the theologians of 2 Kings want to carry us precisely to the abyss between the eighth century of hopelessness and the sixth-century possibility of painful, small steps. It is as though they do not want us to miss the precise way in which it all came about, so that there will be no uncertainty about fault. So we are carried step by step, through one torturous king after another, so that the demise and the descent is clear and unambiguous, unarguable. The theologian must be thinking, "Is that enough; have you caught on yet?" But even in this account which treasures the continuity more than does Isaiah, the end is not different. Either way, gradually in 2 Kings or abruptly as in Isaiah, we are on the way to death.

We may mention in passing yet a third version of the same events. In 2 Chron 32, the same realities are reported, but without such specificity. The report is in guarded language, not very easy to penetrate:

But Hezekiah did not make return according to the benefit done to him, for his heart was proud. Therefore wrath came upon him and Judah and Jerusalem.

The Chronicler stays with his theory that such "pride" must be punished. And yet he must tell the truth.

But Hezekiah humbled himself for the pride of his heart, both he and the inhabitants of Jerusalem, so that the wrath of the Lord did not come upon them in the days of Hezekiah (vv. 25–26).

That is a much more respectful way of saying he had "peace in his time." So the Chronicler struggles with the dilemma. On the one hand he is a good king who should prosper. On the other hand, he is a sell-out who should be punished. And the truth of the matter is a most delicate operation. But the consequence of the sell-out is not denied. He does prosper (vv. 27–30). He does have peace in his time, because he had accommodated himself to imperial realities. But it will not last for his people.

The preacher can have an interesting time of it playing with the varied nuances of the three accounts, in our text, Isa 39–40 and II Chron 32. But in the end, the picture is clear, even if delicate. That is the way it is with all of us who possess any power as the world judges power. We are always set at the edge of accommodation, even when we know better. And so there do come breaks in our history. The breaks are not always evident on the outside, for the world has a way of covering over and denying the discontinuities which are too frightening. But they do come. And when they come, we are never sure if there will be another word of comfort. Like Hezekiah, we are conundrums of pride and humbling. He was one with "pride of heart" (2 Chron 32:25). And he was a man who "humbled himself for the pride of his heart" (v. 26). Well, aren't we all! And that is what makes this story so much our story. We are on both sides of the street when we hear that overriding evangelical promise/threat: "For every one who exalts himself will be humbled, and he who humbles himself will be exalted" (Luke 14:11). In the moves of exalting and humbling, of being prospered and being stricken, there is in some confused way a common pattern between this king who sold out and that other king who had it more clearly: "He humbled himself and became obedient unto death, even death on a cross. Therefore God has highly exalted him" . . . (Phil 2:8–9). Perhaps the difference is that he was exalted by his God and did not exalt himself.

Anyway, this text is about King Hezekiah and not about king Jesus. This narrative shocks our sensitivities to see the outcome of Hezekiah. We "had hoped he would redeem Israel" (Luke 24:21). There was reason for such hope, especially if Isa 9:2–7 is about him, as many believe. It seems that by the shape of the narrative these theologians want to destroy all such problematic hope, to see what lies behind this king. There seems little behind this king, not much stuff out of which to posit hope. Perhaps the theologians mean to say no king will redeem Israel, no king who seeks power and security the way the world gives power and security. Only someone empty-handed, as empty-handed as the torah (cf. Phil 2:6) could redeem Israel. Perhaps the outcome is that even Hezekiah is a false hope. There are few hints given along the way of what a better hope might look like. There is only a waiting.

Manasseh: Underwriter of an Unalterable Future (21:1–26)

The second lead part in this passion presentation toward the death of Jerusalem in 587 B.C. is played by Manasseh, son of Hezekiah. The biblical presentation of him is relatively colorless. Perhaps he is best understood by the contrast he makes to his father Hezekiah and his grandson Josiah. Sandwiched between the two, he is seen as a prototype for historical evil. He is presented in the Bible as an example of the way faithless *historical choice* can lead to *massive disaster*. He is regarded as THE cause of the destruction of 587 (2 Kings 23:12, 26; 24:3; Jer 15:4). Such a character likely will not receive much sermonic attention, except as a foil to his courageous counterparts.

(1) It is worth noting that while he is so vigorously rejected in this theological narrative, he did last on the throne 55 years. That alone suggests considerable stability and some capacity for coping with the Assyrian threat (see 2 Chron 33, which offers a different version of these matters). Indeed, it

may even be suggested that he coped better than Hezekiah. So there is a contrast and perhaps conflict between *the biblical verdict* and the verdict which might be drawn by secular *historians*. A teachable point is the peculiar "politics of obedience" upon which 2 Kings insists.

(2) The narrative report is structured in two characteristic parts. The first part (vv. 1-9) itemizes Manasseh's evil. Clearly he is judged by distinctively religious categories. He violates especially the catalog of prohibitions in Deut 18:9-14. Indeed, perhaps that portion of Deuteronomy has been placed there in anticipation of this king. It will not be useful to focus on the specific offenses. Rather, altogether his actions are a rejection of the torah religion of Israel. This king prefers to trust in the religious manipulations which keeps security for his realm in his own hands. Thus the worship of these other gods is finally technique, a way to manage political reality for our own interests, and at the same time to screen out any critical, transcendent questions. Worth noting is that while the catalog of sins is "religious" in these verses, the addendum of v. 16 reflects *exploitative social practice*. That is a point we might have anticipated. Misdirected religious loyalty results in inhumanity among us.

(3) And the result, again not unanticipated, is the sentence of rejection and death. Yahweh will not tolerate such violations of his own holiness and his commitment to righteousness (vv. 10-15). (To be sure even in these verses it is not all sentence, for there is a return to some of the issues of the indictment.)

The judgment here pronounced on Manasseh is not nearly as concrete as is the indictment. Thus even for all his certitude, this theological historian is a bit subdued in fully characterizing the judgment to come. That judgment is presented in three metaphors which are suggestive but not concrete. The preacher might play with those metaphors.

(a) The judgment will cause "ears to tingle" (v. 12). That distinctive phrase is used only for a reaction of incredulity and revulsion at something beyond decency and possibility (see 1 Sam 3:11; Hab 3:15; Jer 19:3). The preacher will need an imaginative tongue to help the congregation discern the profound and affrontive danger that comes from historical evil. Perhaps we are too numbed, or perhaps we have trivialized evil so that we do not notice. The magnitude of what is anticipated is perhaps like trying to comprehend the Holocaust of six million Jews and the smell of flesh, or the depth of inhumanity in the bombs of Hiroshima and Nagasaki, or the live body count given daily from Vietnam. "Tingling ears" is a response to the reality that God does not blink at evil, but responds to it. This text is only for those in the community who have not succumbed to "the banality of evil."

(b) The second metaphor is the "measuring line" and the "plummet" (v. 13). The intent is obscure. It might mean the reassignment and redistribution of land, so that the present owners will lose and the new owners will be Assyrian (as in the north). An innocent economic practice, when turned to poetic imagery, becomes a devastation. Land loss in such measure is not a normal business transaction. It is more like war, occupation, devastation, revaluation. Our imagination perhaps needs to think about Cuba, China, Zimbabwe, El Salvador where the oppressive regimes yielded not at all, and came to a reckoning. And the reckoning was primarily over land.

(c) The third figure is "a dish wiped clean" (v. 13). Now the theologian uses a domestic image of a wiped out kitchen bowl, signifying emptiness, futility, perhaps famine. There are no full bowls, not even a morsel left, but the holy city now has become a desolation without life-support.

These three images suggest a poet desperate for expression, grasping for phrases beyond convention, for he has been led to speak the un-utterable. That may be too hard a sermon to preach. But the text is clear: disregard of the "politics of obedience" leads to unspeakable devastation, the end of what we thought would never end. Take it publically and perhaps there is a scenario here of the end of political life. Take it personally and each of us may be the fool whose soul is required in the night (Luke 12:15–21).

The two parts of the text (vv. 1–9 as indictment, and vv. 10–16 as sentence) make a very clear contrast when one pays attention to the pronouns. In the first part, it is repeatedly "he, he, he," referring to Manasseh. He is the principle agent. All of that is shifted in vv. 10–16, for now it is all "I, I, I," referring to Yahweh. When history reaches its break point,

Yahweh will be established as the decisive agent. All those who prefer another pronoun will have their deceptive, make-believe history end. For now there is one History-maker who moves in and makes the difference.

(4) What to do with this? I am not sure. It may be too heavy for the church. I think I would handle it without trying to make it "relevant." It is important that Manasseh was not a "bad man," did not intend to be a bad man and had a good intention of ruling effectively. (The alternative tradition of 2 Chron 33:12–13 dares to say he repented.) At the most he drifted into a callous self-serving religion and a calculating autonomous politics. He drifted with it, not knowing what he was doing (Luke 23:34). Thus his disobedience may be unwitting. But the response is nonetheless severe. So these points which might be made:

(a) With such authority and power entrusted to us, we drift into unwitting disobedience to God. And the world may even judge that drift to be "successful."

(b) But God is not fooled by our "successes." There is an answering. The Bible takes human choice seriously; there is a calling to account. This is not "hell-fire and damnation" nor "eternal judgment." It is a claim that historical institutions may be destroyed by unwitting disobedience of torah.

(c) Ironically in vv. 17–18, Manasseh dies peacefully, surely with a "successful funeral," even if it was not a "good death." He left his heirs to answer for his self-serving ways. To them he bequeathed "tingling ears," "a line and a plummet," and "a dish wiped clean." It may be delayed. But the answering is not avoided. Even Josiah could not nullify the future Manasseh had set for his people (23:26).

(5) The note on Amon, son of Manasseh (21:19–25) is a stereotypical repetition of his father. The main move of the narrative is from Manasseh to Josiah. Amon hardly warrants the verses he gets.

Josiah: Repentance/Reform/Betrayal
(22:1—23:30)

In the sweep of this story toward destruction, the abrupt juxtaposition of Hezekiah (18–20) Manasseh (21) and Josiah (22–23) shows the disarray of Judah. King and community

cannot make up their minds, whether to repent and obey, or
to compromise and survive. There is a loss of focus, an uncertainty about the rule of God. The narrative shows a swing to
extremes, with strange mixtures of fidelity and cynicism. The
third of this crucial triad, Josiah, is the model of piety, obedience and success. Preaching about the person and rule of
Josiah might reflect on the urgency and problematic of faithful living. In some ways this is a revisit of the life and faith of
Hezekiah, only the stakes are now more risky.

(1) The Josiah narrative is bounded in 22:2 and 23:25
with the unconditional celebration of this faithful, obedient
man. (The statement parallels that on Hezekiah in 18:5.)
Josiah is singled out, even more than David or Hezekiah, as
the totally torah-oriented man. Josiah's unrivaled virtue is
structurally important to this historian, for it shows the
linkage between *the command of Moses* and *the response of
Josiah* at the beginning and end of the historical recital.
Points to be scored:

   (a) an affirmation: such obedience is possible.
   (b) an implication: obedience of such a powerful one,
       results in well-being for the entire realm.
   (c) a definition: obedience to God is not just good inten-
       tions, but concrete implementation of the torah.
   (d) a question: what forms of obedience are appropriate
       in our own time, given the enormous complicated-
       ness of our society? Certainly this is no petty
       moralism.

As a reflection on this model of faithfulness, attention might
be given to Ps 1 (see Jer 17:5–8) and especially Jer 22:15–16
where Josiah is the practitioner of justice.

(2) The key factor for Josiah and for the entire book of
Kings as now presented is the finding of the torah scroll in
vv. 8–10. (The repair of the temple is incidental to the narrative and subordinate to the finding of the torah scroll.) It is
very late for Judah to avert judgment. This historian shapes
his narrative so that the return to torah is Israel's best, last
chance. The narrative proposes nothing less than a reconstitution of public order and public values according to the torah of Moses. Our society waits for persons with tongues and
imagination and visions of justice to evoke a reordering of
public values. That does not mean to build a nostalgic socie-

ty around Mother's Day, apple pie and Chevrolet. Rather it means raising the fundamental questions of justice and compassion in ways that impinge upon economic interest and political privilege.

I suggest that the finding of the torah evokes two responses which are quite distinct, both of which are important. In vv. 11–20 the narrative tells of the pathos of the king, the personal impact this had upon Josiah. The first action he takes is personal penitence (v. 11) which is characterized as penitence, humbling, rending, weeping (v. 19). We may believe this is not play-acting but the king was suddenly made aware of the unwitting disobedience in which he, after his father, was engaged.

The personal penitence of leadership, the specific "turning" of persons of influence, is basic. We have fallen into a trap of never being sorry enough to change. And leadership has therefore come to mean toughness to the point of cynicism, and never looking back. It boggles the mind to think what might have happened if Richard Nixon had been able genuinely "to rend his heart." Or how differently the world might be shaped if with the fall of the Iranian Shah, the United States had been able to discern its disastrous commitments and make a change. I am moved by the very different style and posture of Willy Brandt, making his way to a Jewish memorial in a death camp, to lead his German people in a genuine act of repentance. The historian understands that new historical possibility can only come with repentance. And repentance means a drastic and dangerous dismantling of our self-sufficiency. New possibility can never come in our own tough cynicism. Josiah shows an alternative, "more excellent way."

(3) But personal turning is irrelevant unless there are concrete public actions. Along with personal repentance, Josiah institutes public reform (23:1–24). He not only confesses his sin but takes action toward a "new and righteous life" in the public realm. It is commonly believed that the scroll found is the book of Deuteronomy in some form. And what Josiah does is to reorder his affairs according to the radical social vision of that text. It would be like a government rediscovering the radical notions of the Declaration of Independence and making that public policy.

The reform of Josiah is a remarkable response to a religious tradition. In that regard it is unlike the various slogans of reform mounted by our political parties, because it is presented as being *disinterested*. Josiah has nothing to gain from this act, but responds to religious authority. Critical scholars suggest it is part of Josiah's political reassertion, but that is not suggested in the text. N. E. Claburn suggests Josiah is more immediately interested in economic gain from the reform. One might ponder the ways in which public policy is predictably a mixture of vested interested and disinterest.

(a) The reform begins with an act of covenanting (23:1–3), with a clarification of public loyalties. This act of covenanting by Josiah is structurally important for 2 Kings. The narrative is shaped to show that Josiah acts for his time as Moses did earlier. This is the new Moses. This people is given a new identity, not just as one of the nations that functions like all the others, but a special people with a different role and identity in history (see Deut 7:6–11). Judah is given a missional identity which had been forgotten. It would be like the United States seriously reentering the dreams and visions of "America the Beautiful." "America the Ugly" is invited to reenter its vision. Or it would be like the modern state of Israel coming to its senses to see it is not a nation state like others, but a special gift in history that lives in other ways. And so for the church—the church drifts into so many accommodations with culture that it forgets the distinctive calling and identity given it (see 1 Cor 1:18–25). Josiah has Israel "consider its call." There will be no church renewal until there is a new clarification of deep loyalties which are radical and singular.

(b) The reform of Josiah focuses on reclaiming of the Jerusalem temple for the torah God, Yahweh (23:4–14). The list of categories is long and tedious. But the list must be rightly understood. It is so long and specific because the apparatus of the temple, complicated as it is, is not just worship equipment, but it is the definer and legitimizer of social policy and social perspective. It is not just liturgic hardware but it forms the "life-world" of Israel. It is in the temple that every society gives expression to its most precious and significant values. And when this symbolization has become trivialized or co-opted to serve special interests, then the worship apparatus functions to pervert genuine religion. That is why, for example, there has been and must be such conflict over American flags in churches, for the flag which began as a gesture for justice and liberty has become (marines and all) a signal for imperialism and exploitation. That is why, in the heavy times of the sixties, black sit-ins went so far as to spit in the eucharist. The elements which anticipate the kingdom come to symbolize destructive hatred and racism. That is the sort of *liturgy-policy issue* that the reform of Josiah addresses.

For a preacher who has the courage, this dismal narrative raises questions about religious symbolism, not only in church but in the high liturgical acts of TV commercials:

...working to keep your trust...

...you're in good hands with...

progress is our most important product...

(c) The reform includes a curious effort in relation to Bethel, the great northern sanctuary (vv. 15–20). While the exact intent is difficult (see 1 Kings 13:2–3), it likely reflects an assertion of independence in the north, a challenge to Assyrian control practiced since 721, i.e., for a century. The historical data is obscure. But if a linkage is made between vv. 4–14 and 15–20, it suggests that a *liberation of religious symbols* has potential for *political liberation* as well.

(d) Josiah's reform finally focuses on Passover (vv. 21–23). Passover is the great engagement of memory in Israel. The festival has fallen into disuse as Israelites were assimilated, grew careless or bored with that concrete memory. A sated, managed society has no need for such a concrete memory, and less and less capacity for such remembering (see Prov 30:9). And for such a society as the one formed by Manasseh, remembering disappears. When the memory is reasserted, it comes as a subversive act, undermining the closed present. Specifically, Passover is a liberation festival, a memory of a time and promise of a time when imperial administration will be made null and void. For the Christian church, this note on the Passover may call us (a) to recover the eucharist as a subversive act of liberation and (b) to embrace more fully Passover which we share with Jews as our proper heritage.

Thus the reform includes:

(i) recovery of radical religious symbols,

    (ii) assertion of political liberty, and
    (iii)recovery of the festival of free memory and liberated
        hope.
And if Jer 22:15–16 is to be trusted, as it surely is, then the
king who reconstituted society turned all his energies to a
new social order of justice and righteousness. The contrast
with Manasseh is total, for that king who practiced syncretism is also the appeaser of Assyria and the shedder of innocent blood (21:16). What Josiah does is to trigger in the life,
politics and imagination of Judah another destiny which Assyria could not envision, tolerate or coopt. For the believing
community, as concerns both church and civil society, the
urgent issue is the *reconstitution of the public order*. But that
requires a *radical theological decision*.

    So the preacher may want to reflect on the linkage and
dialectic of *personal penitence* and *reformed public order*. This
comes close to the issue of "evangelism" and "social action."
Clearly they could not be separated from each other for
Josiah.

    (4) It would be best if the narrative had ended with
23:25. Then things would be tidy and suitably religious. We
would have good sound theology showing that reform is possible. And it works. Indeed it has been promised in 22:20 that
at least the person of the king would be safe.

    But things have gone terribly awry. Events have a way of
not fitting the theory. The narrative does not flinch from the
disclosure of 23:26–30, which seems to contradict the best
possibilities of Josiah. In short order, we are told that
Josiah's efforts are quite inadequate. The evil of Manasseh
has overwhelmed the obedience of Josiah. *All because of Manasseh*, Judah and Jerusalem must be terminated. And as if
that were not enough, Josiah himself is killed in a military
expedition. Josiah's death is a terrible incongruity in Israel
which evokes grief (2 Chron 35:24–25). It is incongruous with
Israel's best theology of obedience and blessing. And no
doubt it is incongruous with the functional theology of middle America. The incongruity concerns the ineffectiveness of
moral passion, the resilient, overriding power of evil and the
seeming futility of battling against it.

    The preachable point may concern human futility—so
why try? Or it may be about God—is it all the same to God,

i.e., Manasseh and Josiah (see Job 9:22; Eccles 9:2)? This narrator should be celebrated at least for his candor. He tells it true and does not blink. But it is as though at the last moment he was forced to renege on the grand theory he had constructed through all this tedious narrative. Life does not make sense at a simple moral level. Repentance fails. Reform fails. What prevails is the politics of power as usual and the religion of relentless evil. Josiah is helpless before Egyptian power and before the legacy of Manasseh. And the narrator is derivatively helpless before the intransigent facts of history. Faith must face that. The faith of the Bible does not exist in a world of pretend.

Without engaging in partisan politics, I suspect the same failure of religious sensibility was in play with the murder of John F. Kennedy. Of all recent presidents, Kennedy did present a sense of vitality, hope and momentum. And then foolishly, incongruously, abruptly, the seeming "good king" is done to death by murder. The congregation must come close at hand to the power of such absurdity.

And so in the book of Kings, where everything is intended to be symmetrical and routine, there is a door opened toward Job. There now are small places for the hazardous question of virtue and reward (see Job 1:9). There is a dreaming awareness that the torah-keepers do not triumph in history. It is only hinted at, not commented on, certainly not resolved. The linkage of virtue and blessing is broken in this very narrative that means to assert it. And so this third element comes as a sobering after Josiah's poignant reputation (23:25) and passionate reform. There is now death not noble. No doubt Josiah was given a grand funeral. But long after that, the terrifying question persists—why try? To this the preacher must address herself. After that death in 609, the narrator would not be the same, nor would Israel. After the death of Kennedy, Patrick Moynihan commented, "We shall laugh again, but we shall not be young again." It was a while before Israel laughed. And being young could only come by being reborn.

Puppets and Pygmies (23:31—25:26)

After the abruptness of Josiah's death in 609 (23:28-30), the rest of the tale of the destruction in 587 is quickly told.

The die is already cast. Now we have only a frantic succession of kings who are no-kings. They follow each other rapidly, but none makes any difference. Even though they are all linked to David, the list is as shabby as was that in the north a century earlier. Everything is settled already with Manasseh (24:3). And the end comes, only lingering a little.

The cast of characters is a series of undistinguished and ineffective heirs of Josiah, all of whom are finally irrelevant. They are helpless in the face of the massive judgment that Yahweh has set in motion. They are indeed pygmies. Not one of them has the stature to make any difference. And they are in fact puppets, either responding to Babylon or, alternatively, seeking help from Egypt. But they are essentially reactors, incapable of taking any initiative, except to accelerate the destruction. Unlike Hezekiah and Josiah, there is no hint of any theological sensitivity. They are irrelevant because they ignore the destiny set by Yahweh.

The historical detail is soon summarized. The narrative gives the impression of only going through the motions for purposes of completeness. It is like naming all the U.S. Presidents in a course on American history to make the list symmetrical. But one would hardly pause over Tyler or Hayes or Harding.

So I suggest two preachable points. First, it is important to focus on the theological claim of the text. It appears to me that it is found in 24:4: "The Lord was not willing to pardon." It is too late. The end is fixed in the face of massive evil, especially with Manasseh. So it is affirmed that God takes evil with utmost seriousness. In this text, though not in every text, there are limits to forgiveness. There is no cheap grace.

Second, I submit the links toward the passion of Jesus are worth considering. This helpless, unimpressive cast of characters is not unlike the band that surrounded Jesus. There also the die is cast and nothing the petty functionaries can do will change that. In our text Jerusalem is destroyed and Israel is exiled. In the passion narrative, it is the Messiah who is killed and with his death the temple is destroyed (Luke 23:45). Is it not asserted in both cases, that finally God will break off his love even for his precious partner? Enough of evil leads to abandonment. Evil causes God-forsakenness,

whether of Israel in exile, of a smoldering temple with none
to save, or a desperate Messiah abandoned on a cross. God-
forsakenness is the sure future of those who mock God. And
the preacher can then explore God-forsakenness, which
comes in more than one mode.

Perhaps some hints of the inexorable movement of God's
judgment is seen in the sequence:

(1) Jehoahaz (23:31–33) is made king in hope of liberation, yet he is helpless in the face of Egypt. He leaves no impact on the realm. He is soon forgotten. At the most he evokes
pathos and grief (see Jer 22:11–12).

(2) Jehoiachim (23:34–24:5), a second son, made a puppet by Pharaoh, is a consummate agent of intrigue, oppression and disobedience. He is remembered by Jeremiah as a
horrendous exploiter (Jer 22:13–15). But so far as the flow of
events is concerned, he also makes no difference.

(3) Jehoiachin, grandson of Josiah (24:6–16), reigns briefly. But he lasts just long enough to pay for the sins of his
family. He is left with an open-ended stretch of years of hopelessness, without any real future (see Jer 22:28–30). In the
contemporary book of Ezekiel, he becomes the criterion by
which exile is reckoned, a sad royal function (see Ezek 1:2).

(4) Zedekiah (24:17–25:7) a third son of Josiah, presides
over the final disarray. Acting as king, he gives a poor show,
for he is not really king. His nephew in Babylon looms over
his shoulder.

All four of these kings are hopeless and helpless. Perhaps
the preacher would want to think about the flow of history,
the work of God's power, the ineffectiveness of human will. If
the analogy is not pressed too closely, one might think of the
ineffective sequence of Kennedy, Johnson, Nixon, Ford, Cart-
er, Reagan—carried by the flow of events, able to tamper
with events but not to make a difference because larger
things are happening which sweep past the governmental apparatus. In our situation, perhaps the analogue is the loss of
world power, whether in the name of oil, or energy or cold
war, or rising expectations in the third world. In any case our
"known world" is in jeopardy. Perchance as for Judah, for us
it slips away and none can halt it.

(5) The end result is destruction and exile (25:8–21). The
temple is gone, repulsively sacked by *goyim* (see Ps 74:4–8).

History is ended. There are no more kings. There is "none to comfort" (Lam 1:9, 16, 17, 21). Our Christian way is to say "the messiah is dead." "We had hoped" (Luke 24:21). But now we do not hope. It is hopeless. It is important to linger there and not rush to resolution. Biblical faith requires that we live fully into that void. This is the null point. Every community of faith knows about that point. Life is indeed experienced that way. The narrative is unflinching in three points:

(a) Life is like that. (b) Life is like that because of evil. God is not mocked. (c) But the narrative is clear: even this decisive nullification happens in the arena of God's rule. The end of the temple, the death of the messiah, are not beyond God's lordship. They are seen rather as signs of the vitality of the one who has been mocked.

(6) The post-collapse arrangement is simply an historical note (25:22–26). But even there the disarray is compounded. For there is still a deathly competition to see who would preside over the ruins. The chagrin of the narrative is that it knows that whoever wins in the scandalous competition has only ruins to govern. The maddening stupidity of Israel is remarkable. The death knell sounds and the ones who are still able, stand at least on their knees in order to kill each other. It is not unlike the disciples on the way to Calvary—quarreling about their future power (Mark 10:35–45)!

A Sign in the Midst of the Nullity (25:27–30)

The last paragraph of the books of Kings is a curious note. It may be only *an historical note* about what came next. As such it may only announce that after thirty-seven years of exile, nevertheless the boy-king Jehoiachin is still alive, still has his identity and yet is under house arrest.

But it is also possible that this is more than an historical note. It may be a *careful and intentional theological assertion* in which the deep and undeniable hope of Israel is reasserted. On that basis, it is argued that the royal promises to David and all the deep hopes of Israel ride on this desolate man. The paragraph is added to show that even Babylon has not crushed Judah's future, because the future lies beyond the grasp of Babylon in the safe hands of God. This little paragraph of hope structurally then off-sets the long, massive narrative of judgment and destruction.

If that is correct, the hope of Israel is given careful and delicate delineation:

(a) There is hope.

(b) Not all the alien power of the empire can crush that hope.

(c) The hope always comes in fragile, precarious ways, always at the brink of being snuffed out.

This king (Messiah) is not quite dead. But he is, like father Abraham, "as good as dead" (Heb 11:12). And so the unutterable power and faithfulness of God are attested in this understated factor. That is how God works, not through the obvious ones, but among those who are judged hopeless by the standards of the world. The ante is of course upped in the New Testament, but the point is the same. It is that this God works new life out of the stuff of death. Jehoiachin is a dead man. Israel is a dead people. And after 2 Kings 25, there is a waiting for the new speech of Ezekiel, a waiting to see if the dead ones will be raised (see Ezek 37:1–14).

The text offers to the congregation a ground for hope which may be as subversive as it is untenable. If this paragraph claims so much, then it is asserted that neither the aggressiveness of imperial power nor the evil of God's own people can finally thwart God's good purpose. Hope beyond history is asserted, but a hope born only in the midst of history:

> God's truth abideth still,
> His kingdom is forever (see Isa 14:24–27).

Bibliography

Brueggemann, Walter, *Prophetic Imagination* (Philadelphia: Fortress Press, 1978).

Bryce, Glendon, *A Legacy of Wisdom* (Lewisburg: Bucknell University Press, 1979).

Buber, Martin, *The Prophetic Faith* (New York: Harper and Brothers, 1949).

Childs, Brevard, *Introduction to the Old Testament as Scripture* (Philadelphia: Fortress, 1979).

Childs, Brevard, *Isaiah and the Assyrian Crisis* (SBT 32; Naperville: Alec R. Allenson, Inc., 1967).

Ellul, Jacques, *The Politics of God and the Politics of Man* (Grand Rapids: Eerdmans, 1972).

Maly, Eugene, *The World of David and Solomon* (Englewood: Prentice-Hall, 1966).

McCarthy, Dennis J., *Kings and Prophets* (Milwaukee: Bruce Publishing Co., 1968).

Mendenhall, George, "The Monarchy," *Interpretation* 29 (1975) 155–170.

Napier, B. Davie, *Word of God, Word of Earth* (Philadelphia: United Church Press, 1976).

Niebuhr, Reinhold, *Irony in American History* (New York: Scribner, 1952).

von Rad, Gerhard, *Studies in Deuteronomy* (SBT 9; Chicago: Henry Regnery Co., 1953).

Westermann, Claus, *Handbook to the Old Testament* (Minneapolis: Augsburg Publishing House, 1967).

Wolff, Hans Walter, "The Kerygma of the Deuteronomic Historical Work," in *The Vitality of Old Testament Traditions* by Walter Brueggemann and Hans Walter Wolff (Atlanta: John Knox Press, 1975) 83–100.